Stories From Around
the World 2

Stories From Around the World 2

Edited by
Keith Danby

Authentic
LIFESTYLE

First published in 2003 by Authentic Lifestyle

09 08 07 06 05 04 03   7 6 5 4 3 2 1

Authentic Lifestyle is an imprint of
Authentic Media
PO Box 300, Carlisle, Cumbria, CA3 0QS, UK
and PO Box 1047, Waynesboro, GA 30830-2047, USA
www.paternoster-publishing.com

British Library Cataloguing in Publication Data
A catalogue record for this book is available from the
British Library

ISBN 1-85078-531-7

Cover design by STL Design and Production
Printed in Great Britain by
Cox and Wyman Ltd., Reading

Contents

Introduction

How much can you buy for one British pound? Two litres of petrol? A McDonald's breakfast muffin and a drink? A bag of fries or a hamburger at your local carryout? A Mars bar, packet of crisps and a coke at the convenience store? Or a bargain or remainder book at your nearest discount bookshop? Actually, it's a struggle to think of too much more.

Yet I am sure you have heard it said many times that from little acorns grow huge oak trees. Several years ago a seed of thought of producing a book, the proceeds from which would go to support Christian mission projects around the world, was planted. At the time I have to confess my ambition was relatively small. I wondered . . . if we sold the book for £1 and if we could sell 5000 copies, we could then raise £5000 for some needy causes. And so the seed of thought germinated and began to grow.

The authors were approached, the stories began to come together and the cover and the marketing plan were agreed. The publication date had been set for 19 September 2002, but even before this date I realised we were on to something special, as the pre-publication orders began to come in. The print run grew from 5000 to 10,000, then the 10,000 was increased 20,000, and finally we signed off on 30,000, as Christian retailers and distributors seemed to catch the vision behind the concept.

The next big challenge was to keep track of the sales and make sure we did not run out of stock. Inevitably, we had to reprint on several occasions, each time with a little more courage. We had decided that the cut-off date would be 31 January 2003, for no other reason than it coincided with the financial year end of our charity – Send the Light Limited. I am delighted to say that by this date the sales had reached 63,000 copies and had raised $100,000.

The book climbed to the UK Christian Bestsellers No. 1 position, with many retailers, including the Wesley Owen Books and Music and Christian Literature Crusade chains, selling the book for £1 at zero profit. Some retailers even used it as a promotional giveaway.

The next big task was for the STL Trust to decide how to disperse the funds. As chairman I suggested the money should be used for both UK and international projects and that particular consideration should be given to some of the organisations featured in the book. It was also agreed that we would continue to follow the broad guidelines of the STL Trust, which supports Bible training and education, evangelism and social action and relief projects.

The fruit from this little book of stories has spread across the globe. Cash grants were given to **Signpost International** to support its housing projects in the Philippines and its work among street children in Brazil. Several projects were linked to Africa. Two students from Uganda training for the ministry at the **International Christian College** in Glasgow were sponsored. A HIV/Aids project designed to produce literature to help educate nationals on how to prevent this deadly disease spreading further – a particular burden of mission leader **George Verwer** – was supported. A gift to help an orphanage in Malawi, which cares for children of Aids victims, and support for a job creation scheme, which opened a small retail outlet on the outskirts of Cape Town, was given.

Money was donated to help buy books for students training for the ministry in northern India. Support was given to **The Bethany Hospital** – a community hospital just outside Mumbai (formerly known as Bombay), which has grown rapidly in the last ten years and seeks to give free or subsidised medical care to some of the poorest of the poor in that mega-city. Support was also given to a project several thousand miles north of Mumbai in the state of Gujarat, ravaged by a massive earthquake in January 2001, which killed an estimated 100,000 people and left hundreds of thousands of survivors without homes, food or clean drinking water. In response, many relief agencies have co-operated to try and rebuild some of the small villages. **OM India**, working together with World Relief and the Delhi Discipleship Centre, has concentrated its efforts on a number of Dalit villages. The Dalit people group is regarded as the lowest of all the Indian castes and its members are sometimes referred to as the 'untouchables'. The relief agencies were committed to build 'earthquake-proof' housing, schools and community centres in at least three villages. The contribution from *Stories* has helped to pay for one of the schools.

This all seemed like an eggcup of water in a desert or like five small loaves and two sardines when there are so many hungry people to satisfy. Our confidence, however, is not in what seem hopelessly meagre amounts, but in the person of Jesus Christ, who delights to take what we give him and use it to make a difference. We will never meet or perhaps even hear about these people, but God knows.

In the UK some twenty projects received support, many connected with youth evangelism in schools in communities reaching from Woking in the south of England to Carlisle in the north. There were two organisations in Scotland, one in Hamilton and the other in East Kilbride, also working in schools and with children, that were supported. In addition there was support for the **Scottish Bible Society**'s exciting Bible World Exhibition, which attracts thousands of visitors each week, many of them schoolchildren visiting as part of a school trip.

There were two projects in London that were helped: an Oasis International **Faithworks** initiative in Southwark and an OM **Turning Point** project, which seeks to provide a centre to offer friendship to the thousands of Muslims who either live in the city or visit as tourists each year.

What does church look like in twenty-first-century Britain? Well, if you live in Bristol or Carlisle, it might look very different from what happens most Sundays in many of our cities, towns and villages. There is a new Christian community project in Bristol called **Hope Community Church**. I visited this project with my good friend Rob Parsons, of Care for the Family. The leaders took us to a young offender institution. As we met some of the young people and sat in their cells, it was a heart-wrenching experience to hear their stories and learn about their backgrounds. Many of them were in their early teens, without Christ and without hope. Hope Community Church works with the chaplains and some Christian volunteers who bring the good news of Jesus Christ to the inmates, many of whom have nowhere to go when they are released and often end up back in trouble within a few days of being back on the 'outside'. Amidst the darkness and despair, there was a flicker of hope, as these faithful servants of Christ lead Alpha courses and supply Christian resources, but mainly express the love of Jesus to these desperately needy young people. Further north, in Carlisle, there is the **Living Well** project. Here, church is in a double-decker bus, driven around the Rattles Estate. The workers do not use the Prayer Book or even sing the latest worship songs. Their congregation have never heard of Graham Kendrick or Matt Redman, can barely read and have never read Philip Yancey or even J. John – sorry, guys! But Living Well is just like it sounds. It is providing streams of living waters in an inner-city housing estate, which is an urban desert.

And there is more! Support was given for the music band The Tribe and their work with **Message Ministries**, and for **Noel Richard**s and a concert in Slovakia. Help too was offered for literature translation in Eastern Europe through **EELAC** and the **Overseas Centre for Mission Studies** in Oxford and finally **Keswick Ministries**, bringing God's word and teaching to the UK and overseas.

So, what you can buy for a pound? A whole new life!

In *Stories From Around the World* 2 we want to carry on the good work started by *Stories from*

Around the World. This book provides many more inspiring stories from around the world and once again I am grateful to the authors of the stories and their publishers for agreeing to their inclusion. In addition, we have produced a CD with worship songs from around the world. These products, together with the original book, *Stories from Around the World*, will be available and once again the proceeds will be used to support many more exciting projects around the world. This time, with my faith enlarged and my vision increased, I would like to raise even more! May God grant this prayer.

Keith Danby
Group Chief Executive
Send the Light

ROB PARSONS

Rob Parsons is an international speaker on business and family issues. He has spoken to more than 300,000 people in seminars around the world and his books, including bestsellers such as *The Sixty Minute Father*, *The Sixty Minute Marriage* and *Bringing Home the Prodigals*, have sold approaching half a million copies in ten languages.

Rain in the Desert: The Power of Appreciation

by Rob Parsons

Many years ago, I was taken by a guide into the Sinai desert. It was a fascinating journey, and one experience remains as vivid in my mind as the moment it happened. The guide stopped the jeep and showed me a very special bush. He told me that this plant had a rare ability that ensured its survival in that hostile environment. Quite simply, it had learned to live with very little water. When times of drought came, other vegetation would quickly wither, but this one died in sections. If no rain came, perhaps half of it would close down, and the rest was able to use whatever moisture it could find. And then, as the drought progressed, it would close other parts down, until finally there might be just a single stem waiting for the rain. And when the rain came, the seed pods on that stem would explode and send new life bursting into the desert again.

I have seen the same principle at work in my life and in the lives of others when it seems that life, faith and hope have just dried up and we hang on by the skin of our teeth and pray that the rain will come again. And I have seen it in marriage. You can observe it when men and women become starved of self-worth and they crave again somebody to show them that they matter. This longing is so deep that if it doesn't come eventually from their partner, it may be that they will find that appreciation in an affair.

I was sitting in a crowded cafe; on a nearby table, a woman sat alone. As we ate, there was a constant stream of people looking for seats. A man came to the table that she occupied and said, 'Is this place free – are you alone?' She said, 'I'm always alone.' I have tried to imagine what was going on in her life that had made her reach out to a total stranger with such a plea, and such an invitation.

Knowing that we matter

Dr James Dobson set out to identify the reasons for periods of depression in women. He had observed that, in counselling sessions with women of varying ages and backgrounds, the same frustrations were mentioned. He devised a ten-item questionnaire, which listed the themes that had so often been mentioned as the cause of depression. The women were asked to rank the ten items according to their frustration from each source. The most depressing was to be given a 1; the least relevant item scored a 10. The participants were married women between the ages of twenty-seven and forty years – the average age was thirty-two. The majority were mothers who still had small children at home. They were asked to fill in the chart anonymously. You might like to try it:

Irritant	Rank
Absence of romantic love in my marriage	1
In-law conflict	2
Low self-esteem	3
Problems with the children	4
Financial difficulties	5
Loneliness, isolation and boredom	6
Sexual problems in marriage	7
Menstrual and physiological problems	8
Fatigue and time pressure	9
Ageing	10

We have spoken over the past years to tens of thousands of couples on the issue of marriage, had countless conversations and read and answered hundreds of letters. Having done all of that, I am not surprised at the results of Dr Dobson's survey, because I have seen the same results time after time. The majority of those women chose 'Low self-esteem' as the greatest difficulty in their lives.

Low self-esteem is something that can hit any man, woman, or child; and in some it actually becomes a terminal illness. I can best describe it by telling you about a school photograph that made me cry.

It was of a large group of children at the beginning of their teen years. The girls were already looking like women in the making; the boys were looking like – well, large boys. But one girl caught my attention. She was very overweight and sat with her hands on her knees. She did not have a pretty face, but she smiled out from behind thick spectacles. I asked my friend's child to tell me about her.

Apparently, she had few friends because, among other things, she smelled a little and some of the children would not sit by her. She was not good at sport and regularly came somewhere near the bottom of the class in terms of academic achievement. Whenever the teacher asked two leaders to pick teams, she was always the last one chosen, and invariably one captain would say, 'You can have her.'

And as I looked at her, I felt a great emotion well up in me. I wanted to hold her, to tell her she was wonderful, that she was *somebody*. I wanted to find something in that child's life that she could do moderately well and praise her for it. I wanted to tell her that I would always be her friend, that I would love to sit by her.

That child was like a plant in the desert waiting for the rain, but there seemed no hope that anybody – teacher, friend, perhaps even a parent – would come over the horizon and say, 'I appreciate you.' As I have recounted that incident at some of our seminars, people have come to me and said something like this: 'I'm forty years old . . . I have a responsible job . . . I have three lovely children . . . but I understand that girl in the photograph . . . it's how I feel right now.' As human beings, we need to know that we matter to somebody almost as much as we need breath.

One of the best-selling management books of all time is a slim volume called *The One Minute Manager.* You can buy it on any railway station for just a few pounds, and yet many employers say that the principles contained in it have revolutionised their workplace. So what great secrets of wisdom lie in the pages of this book that can so change the way that organisations work? It's not difficult. The author says, 'Learn to appreciate people; learn to praise.' He says that if we took just sixty seconds a week to show our appreciation of those who work for us, we would see incredible changes in attitudes, relationships and even productivity. I believe he is right, and I think that way because the principles contained in that book are not new; in fact, they are very old and are contained in a much older book and are based on the fact that we are created in the image of God – that each of us has dignity and we are meant to recognise that in each other. The issue of appreciation, of giving each other worth, is a crucial one in any relationship, but it is rain in the desert to a marriage that is dying.

Over the years we have seen many marriages fall into an ever-deepening spiral of despair. Many things have contributed to that, and for some there comes a time when they say, 'I've had enough; it's over.' But we have sometimes observed a strange thing happen. Something seems suddenly to kick that tired, old, almost-dead love into life again. Time and time again the ingredient that does this is appreciation. One of the partners decides, almost as an act of the will, to appreciate the other. It is as if they say to themselves, 'I will not go on taking my husband/wife for granted; I will show that I care.' The fascinating thing is that the decision is so often not born out of the emotions of the feeling of love, but out of sheer will power to initiate change. And so they begin in little ways to show that the other person matters, and they find that they have unleashed one of the most powerful agents of change in human relationships: the power of praise – the secret of appreciation.

Mark Twain understood that; he said, 'I can live for two months on a sincere compliment.'

In many marriages a partner has to live for thirty years without any real demonstration of appreciation. You can have a home with every labour-saving device imaginable, you can have a prestigious job or the kind of face and figure that make the models on the catwalks look boring, but you will die inside without knowing that you matter to somebody.

What am I worth?

It is fascinating how we evaluate whether we have worth in the eyes of another person – whether or not our partner appreciates us. I once asked Dianne, 'Darling, if you could change anything at all about me, what would it be?' I had rather hoped that Di would have to think about it for a while, but she didn't even hesitate. 'Rob,' she said, 'when you shave, you always leave the stubble around the sink; and I'm not sure how you do it, but you get the shaving foam up the wall – higher than head-height! And when you've finished, you roll the towel into a wet ball and throw it into the bath!' (I was now wondering what was coming next, and had a facial expression which my children call 'gobsmacked'.) Dianne went on: 'I would like you to remove the stubble and the shaving foam, fold the towel up and put it over the radiator.'

I managed to get my jaw back into gear and spluttered, 'Is that it?'

Di replied, 'That will do for starters!'

I have thought so much about that incident. Why was that such a big deal to Dianne? I think I know the answer to that now. You see, although Di has had various jobs outside the home, just then she was a full-time homemaker, and she was looking at the devastation in the bathroom and wanting to say something like this to me: 'Rob, just now my job is in this home. When I clean, when I try the picture on this wall instead of that one, when I put things in their right place – that is part of my main task right now. They may seem small things, and be assured there are days when I'd rather be advising the Cabinet on some intricate economic problem. More than that, it's from the job of homemaker that at the moment I get a large chunk of my identity. And when you and the children come home and leave the place as though hurricane Flora has just visited us, it's as if you're saying to me, "What you do doesn't matter." And Rob, I sometimes feel that what you're saying is, "What you are doesn't matter."'

These may seem such small issues, but if we are to begin to learn the power of appreciation, it's probably at the basics that we need to begin. It is so easy to convey to another person by our everyday attitudes that they don't really matter to us.

We came across a moving prayer the other day. It came from the lips of a woman who craves to be somebody in the eyes of those she loves:

> Lord, I don't feel loved any more, I don't feel wanted. My children demand so much of me and take it without appreciation. They overlook the things they could do for me and when I ask for their help, they cruelly rebel. My husband is too preoccupied with problems even to suspect this awful vacancy I feel. I scarcely know my neighbours and my friends are too busy with their own concerns to really care.
>
> Who would care, Lord, if I disappeared tomorrow? Who would really care? I know that I am needed, and for that reason alone I would be missed. But wanted, Lord, really wanted as a person, for myself?
>
> You, Lord, you alone know and love and care about me as a person. In you alone I find my understanding and reassurance.
>
> Oh, give us all back reassurance.
>
> Let us feel loved and wanted.

'I find it so hard to show appreciation'

Why do so many of us find it hard to give appreciation and praise? Much of it has to do with taking others for granted. I remember my first bicycle. It had three gears, a saddlebag and white pedals (whoever designed a boy's bike with *white pedals*?). I loved that bike. Whenever I'd finished riding it, I would clean it, making sure that all the rain was dried off and then, when I had finished the frame, I would turn my attention to the pedals. I was determined to keep them 'Persil' white. That kind of attention was a nine-day wonder. Two things conspired to destroy it: firstly, I just got used to that bike. When it was in the shop window, its very distance made it seem mysterious, but there wasn't much mystery about hitting my leg on it ten times a day as it stood in the little hallway at home. But, secondly, one day I saw Martin Harrison's bike: it had ten gears! Mine seemed a boring old affair by comparison.

So it is in our relationships. We begin with such promise, such excitement, as if our whole married life is to be one great big Gold Blend coffee advert. And then we begin to get used to each other. It may even be that the things that attracted us now annoy us. What we used to call 'strong' we now call 'stubborn', the gentle personality that had so attracted us we now call 'weak'. Such a taking for granted is a tragedy, and for so many it is not until the marriage is broken and we have lost that person that we begin to realise what good characteristics they had, and how we just got used to them. At the time, it seemed tremendously important that they be thinner, or better around the house, or stronger with the children. But now we remember that they were kind, or warm, that they always had time for us, and we never appreciated it.

Sometimes we find it hard to show appreciation because we have never received it. Many of us have never known a parent's praise. After one of our seminars a middle-aged man came up to me. He told me that he remembers running home from school, having come top in a music exam for the whole of his county. He got ninety-seven per cent. He ran into the house. 'Dad, Dad, I came top, I got ninety-seven per cent!'

His father said, 'Won't you ever get full marks?'

This man was very successful in his career; others looked at him and wished they could be like him, but he represents the many men and women who in adult life are still pursuing the approval of the father or mother they could never please. They may have lived under the shadow of a more clever or athletic brother or sister, and they crave appreciation for what they are in themselves.

Think back for a moment to the little girl in the school photograph. The day may come when she will be a mother. How will she be with her children? Wouldn't you think that she would vow never to put her own children through what she knew? Wouldn't you think that she

would resolve never to say to her child in public, 'Hey, look what the cat dragged in,' that she
would build her children up at every opportunity? The sadness is that she may well treat her
children as she was treated. She never received
praise and appreciation, and she may find it
hard to give it. And that destructive pattern of
behaviour may mean she will never say to her
husband, 'I am so proud of you, thank you for
what you have done.'

Another reason that many of us find it so
hard to praise is because we feel so insecure
ourselves. In fact we find it easier to bring others down, as if that very act elevates us. So often
that shows itself in the way we talk to our
partner. We may delight in criticising them in
public or making jokes about their weight or
cooking ability. In the home, we may find that
we enjoy pointing out where they have gone
wrong, or use our tongue as a weapon of
destruction.

Destroying self-esteem

Mark and Rachel had known a good marriage.
They were in their mid-thirties, had two children and seemed happy. But in reality there
was something eating at the heart of this relationship like a cancer. By the time they agreed
to counselling, it seemed the marriage was all

but over. What had caused that? There were certainly many of the normal problems. They had long since stopped talking to each other. It wasn't that they didn't communicate – they did – but they didn't really say anything. Any in-depth talk about how they really felt was gone. Then there was the busyness that had slowly but systematically choked the love out of this marriage because it stifled it of the one thing it needed to grow: time. There were other common themes that had all played their part in the death of love, but in the middle of them all, one stood out. By no means did it seem at first sight to be the greatest reason, and yet as I listened to them I became convinced that this, above all, had killed the love of that woman for her husband. It was his tongue.

It was a tongue that over the years had been used to bring her down. Sometimes it would be at a party, when it would be a jibe about her weight. If they entertained, it would be a joke about the meal. He would laugh, the guests would smile awkwardly, thinking, 'Why doesn't she throw it over him?' and she would die inside – again.

And that was what had happened: slowly, word by word, over the years of their marriage, he had killed the dignity and the self-worth, the sense of being somebody in that woman. And finally, he had put to death the feeling that he was somebody to her.

She was in her seventies, had beautiful silvery hair and a lovely dignity about her which made it hard to understand the story that she told me. She had been married twice and she told me that her first husband had killed her love for him with his tongue. She said, 'He would say to me almost every day, "You cow!"' She told me that she took that abuse day after day. She said that single phrase had summed up how he had treated her — as if she were less than a person. And after a while she began to believe it. But then one day, in the middle of another barrage, which again ended with the usual phrase, a thought came to her. She said to herself, 'Cows aren't such bad creatures; you get milk from cows, you get leather from cows; cows are good parents.' The next time he began his abuse, she replied, 'Cows aren't so bad; you get milk from cows, leather from cows; cows are good parents.' And then she turned to me and with a twinkle in her eye said, 'He never called me that again!'

And I have so often seen a husband who feels he is not appreciated. It may be that he says, 'I just bring home the money. Nobody ever says, "Thanks. Thanks, Dad, for the holiday, thanks for the jacket, thank you for all that you do for us." I'm just a meal ticket.' Appreciation is especially vital when unemployment hits a home. I have observed similar symptoms in a man or woman robbed of their job as in bereavement. It is vital at such times that the family let them know they have dignity in the home and are appreciated, irrespective of their ability to bring home money. They must know they are valued for *who they are*.

Six keys to appreciation

1 Create in others a sense of worth

When we show appreciation to anybody, we give them dignity, and it is especially so in the family. We need to let each other know in a hundred different ways that we are appreciated – that we matter.

My late father used to find it so hard to give praise, but my mother worked overtime at it. Our home was poor; we didn't have luxuries like an inside toilet, or a bathroom, or even running hot water, and I had friends who seemed to be a lot better off, but she gave me something that money cannot buy: a sense of value. Even now, I remember something she said to me in my mid-teens: 'Rob, I know that you have to mix with kids who have more money than we do, but I want you to know that you are as good as anybody; you are not better than others, treat all with respect – but you are special to me and I believe in you. I have saved some money

– you and I will call it "the bank" – it's in a tin on top of the landing cupboard. If ever you need money, you must come to me and we will go to the bank together.'

It wasn't until I was twenty-two years old that I discovered that the bank had never existed. How could it? She had so little money. But she tried so hard to give me, in her way, a sense of value.

It is vital in marriage that we give a sense of dignity to each other.

2 *Practise the power of praise*

Catch yourself when you are about to give some piece of carping criticism or hurtful comment. I was counselling a couple who, as they spoke, would each bring the other down. At one stage the husband said, 'My wife is obsessed with the thought of our daughter leaving home.'

I stopped him and said, 'Try saying that differently. Try saying, "My wife is so concerned about our daughter when she leaves home and how she will cope."'

Then I asked the wife to tell me any characteristic in her husband of which she was proud. She mentioned his reliability and utter consistency, and I saw him gaze at her. It had been years since he had heard praise from her lips. They had spent ten years bringing each other down, playing the dignity-destroying game of verbal volleyball. They were experiencing something written in the book of Proverbs by one of the wisest men who ever lived: 'A crushed spirit dries up the bones.' But it was not too late for them to discover the life-changing power of praise.

3 Develop the touch of appreciation

Touch is a powerful tool for conveying to somebody that you appreciate them and give them worth. Some of the most amazing words in the New Testament are spoken of Jesus when he was faced with a leper. The man had the most humiliating of diseases, which prevented him from talking, and even worshipping, with family and friends. In fact, the nearest those who loved him had reached was a few hundred yards as they heard the bell he carried to warn people away. He must have felt he was at the bottom of the pile. And then 'Jesus touched him'. It may be that the man had not felt a human touch for many years, but here was this young teacher giving him such dignity. Jesus spoke to him, he needed that; he made him well, and he had prayed for that; but before he healed him, Jesus had touched him.

It is so in our families. Meaningful touch is a crucial way of communicating appreciation and love. F B. Dressler, in *The Psychology of Touch*, maintains that women in particular need eight to ten meaningful touches each day just to maintain emotional and physical health. The role of touch in marriage is often quite different for men and women. Men often associate touch with sex, but a wife will often crave for touch which demonstrates not interest in sexual intercourse, but interest in her. A man may say to his wife, 'You never come up to me in the kitchen and put your arms around me any more.' His wife will reply, 'No, because if I do, within five minutes you'll expect me to be diving into bed.' We need to develop touch which does not automatically lead to the bedroom, but which affirms the other person.

The messages that touch gives are at least as powerful as what we say. It could be a father putting his hand on a son's head to convey to him, 'Son, I am so proud of you'; or a wife squeezing a husband's arm as he leaves for a difficult meeting, to say, 'I'm with you in all of this.' It could be that a husband will reach out an arm in bed just to hold his wife. Those simple actions can change our relationships, but, just as with good verbal communication, they don't just happen, and we normally need a little practice!

In our culture, and particularly for men, touch often does not come naturally. It's important, of course, that we find what suits us in our marriage, but it's as well not just to say, 'Oh, I'm not the emotional type!' Touch is powerful, and we need it at all ages. A boy of thirteen said to us recently, 'My parents have stopped hugging me now I'm a teenager, but when nobody else was looking, I wish they still would.' I heard of a woman in her late seventies. She lived alone, and once a week took lessons in ballroom dancing. Somebody asked her if she loved dancing. She said, 'Oh, I enjoy it, but the real reason I go is that it's the only time that anybody touches me.'

4 Find the `keys to appreciation'

One of the most sobering things about being involved in marriage counselling is to realise how different we all are in our marriage relationships. Some years ago a book was published giving ways to revitalise your marriage. It included tips such as the wife dressing in a skimpy nightie and flinging herself into the husband's arms as he came home from work. The author could never have had children. We can just imagine the romance routine being interrupted by a three-year-old saying, 'Mummy – quick – the cat's got the hamster . . . and why are you dressed for bed?'

The ways that we can express appreciation meaningfully will differ, but in every marriage there will be 'keys to appreciation' – ways in which your partner perceives whether or not you care. Let's say right now that the 'formal' occasions such as birthdays, anniversaries and Valentine's Day are important, but just as vital is the way that appreciation is expressed in the everyday.

The secret of the 'keys to appreciation' is that these things are important to your partner, not necessarily to you. When Lloyd was very young, I bought him as a Christmas present a very complicated Meccano set. I loved it! In other words, I gave him what I thought he needed. 'Keys to appreciation' are different. They may be small, but they say to our partner, 'I know that this matters to you.'

When we hear some of them from the marriages of others, they may sound corny, but they work for them. Let me give you a few of ours. As far as Dianne is concerned, she appreciates flowers and little gifts, and I suppose if I told her that I had booked the Orient Express to take us on a romantic tour with Cliff Richard singing as we went, she'd be grateful. But nothing works like saying, 'Don't do a meal tonight; we'll all get fish and chips – or I'll cook it.' (Kids seen leaving with packed suitcases!) For me, it's when she says, 'Take some time out for yourself – go off for the day kick the leaves – we'll all try to survive until you get back!' Those moments of personal space say to me,

'My wife cares enough to know I need that time.'

Your keys will be different. It could be not walking past dirty washing on the landing, or helping with some paperwork. These are not world-shattering issues, but they are meaningful in your relationship.

Let me give you some I have heard from other marriages:

Filling the car with petrol and checking the tyres.

Giving your partner a 'cooking-free' day. They don't even have to think about food.

Saying, 'This evening is yours – do with it what you want. I'm holding the fort!'

Cuddling in bed (without unbridled passion breaking out!).

Noticing when the house has been 'extra cleaned.' Making the bed before leaving for work.

Saying, 'You go to bed - I'll bring up a drink - get lost in a book.'

Not passing socks, shoes or old cups of tea without picking them up.

Listening – taking the phone off the hook when your partner has something to share that's important to them.

Gritting your teeth and saying, 'Darling, if you want to go there that much, I wouldn't want to miss it for the world.'

5 *Take a second look*

It's so easy to major on the parts of our partner's character or physical appearance that we don't like. It can sometimes be helpful to take time to consider the positive qualities that we do find attractive. I fully understand that in some marriages the relationship has so broken down that at least one of the partners will say, 'There is absolutely nothing that I like about my partner.' The interesting thing is that often after divorce a partner will look back and say, 'I know I didn't love her at the end, but looking back, I can see qualities she had, that if I'm honest, I miss now. It was just so hard to think clearly at the time.'

Take a few minutes to consider some of those qualities. Go on – you may just find something that you appreciate!

Something my partner has achieved or made that I admire . . .

Something I like about my partner's appearance . . .

Something practical I'm glad my partner does really well . . .

The quality I most like about my partner is . . .

My partner has put up with me in these areas . . .

6 'Let the good times roll!'

The mind is a fascinating thing. It has the ability to recall events and sometimes block them out. Generally, we look back on the past in a kindly way. That's why, years ago, the summers were always hotter, the Christmases more 'Christmassy', and the police more helpful. We can easily fool ourselves if we always wear those rose-tinted spectacles. That's why the book of Ecclesiastes has that fascinating verse: 'Do not say, "Why were the old days better than these?" For it is not wise to ask such questions.' But the mind can also play an opposite trick on us. When relationships with others are hard, it seems to have the ability to block out the memories of the good times. We forget the time when they stood by us; we cannot recall the years when the relationship was so fulfilling, when we felt so very blessed.

It's a good idea to make a note of moments in our marriage which have been special to us. It could be a holiday, or the experiences learned together during a child's illness. It may be a little kindness that lifted us when we needed it, or memories of hilarious laughter. It's good to record those occasions, because in times of difficulty we so quickly forget the good things. And it can be at times, when it seems that love has died, and there is no hope for us, that the scanning of those old memories begins the flicker of feeling in us and raises at least the possibility that love could grow again and we could be 'the way we were'.

Take what is helpful here; use what works for you. But let none of us say, 'Oh, I don't need to say anything or demonstrate by actions – she knows I love her.' That philosophy is a hundred per cent wrong. The only way we can tell if we are valued and loved is by what people say and do. Love says, 'This is how much I appreciate you, and even if love seems hard to feel at the moment, then as an act of the will, I will appreciate you.' When we are valued like that, it is life-changing, it affects our very personalities, because it answers the deepest question a man or woman can ask: 'Do I have real worth?'

All that I have tried to say here is so clearly illustrated in one of my favourite stories. It's from a culture that seems strange to us, but the lesson at the heart of it universal.

* * *

Johnny Lingo and the Eight-Cow Wife

It took the sharpest trader on the islands to realise the cheapest deal isn't always the best bargain

The time I sailed to Kiniwata, an island off the Japanese coast, I took along a notebook. After I got back it was filled with descriptions of the flora and fauna, native customs and costumes. But the only note that still interests me is the one that says: 'Johnny Lingo gave eight cows to Sarita's father.' And I don't need to have it in writing. I'm reminded of it every time I see a woman belittling her husband or a wife withering under her husband's scorn. I want to say to them, 'You should know why Johnny Lingo paid eight cows for his wife.'

Johnny Lingo wasn't exactly his name. But that's what Shenkin, the manager of the guesthouse on Kiniwata, called him. Shenkin was from Chicago and had a habit of Americanising the names of the islanders. But Johnny was mentioned by many people in many connections.

If I wanted to spend a few days on the neighbouring island of Nurabandi, Johnny Lingo could put me up. If I wanted to fish, he could show me where the biting was best. If it was pearls I sought, he would bring me the best buys. The people of Kiniwata all spoke highly of Johnny Lingo. Yet when they spoke they smiled, and the smiles were slightly mocking.

'Get Johnny Lingo to help you find what you want and let him do the bargaining,' advised Shenkin. 'Johnny knows how to make a deal.'

'Johnny Lingo!' A boy seated nearby hooted the name and rocked with laughter.

'What's going on?' I demanded. 'Everyone tells me to get in touch with Johnny Lingo, then falls about laughing. Let me in on the joke.'

'Oh, the people like to laugh,' Shenkin said, shrugging. 'Johnny's the brightest, the strongest young man in the islands. And, for his age, the richest.'

'But if he's all you say, what is there to laugh about?

'Only one thing. Five months ago, at the festival, Johnny came to Kiniwata and found himself a wife. He paid her father eight cows!'

I knew enough about island customs to be impressed. Two or three cows would buy a fair to middling wife, four or five a highly satisfactory one.

'Good Lord!' I said. 'Eight cows! She must have beauty that takes your breath away.'

'She's not ugly,' he conceded and smiled a little. 'But the kindest could only call Sarita plain. Sam Karoo, her father, was afraid she'd be left on his hands.'

'But then he got eight cows for her? Isn't that extraordinary?

'Never been paid before.'

'Yet you call Johnny's wife plain?

'I said it would be kindness to call her plain. She was skinny. She walked with her shoulders hunched and her head ducked. She was scared of her own shadow.'

'Well,' I said, 'I guess there's just no accounting for love.'

'True enough,' agreed the man. 'And that's why the villagers grin when they talk about Johnny. They get special satisfaction from the fact that the sharpest trader in the islands was outwitted by dull old Sam Karoo.'

'But how?

'No one knows and everyone wonders. All the cousins were urging Sam to ask for three cows and hold out for two until he was sure Johnny'd pay only one. Then Johnny came to Sam Karoo and said, 'Father of Sarita, I offer eight cows for your daughter.'

'Eight cows,' I murmured, 'I'd like to meet this Johnny Lingo.'

I wanted fish. I wanted pearls. So the next afternoon I beached my boat at Nurabandi. And I noticed as I asked directions to Johnny's house that his name brought no sly smile to the lips of his fellow Nurabandians. And when I met the slim, serious young man, when he welcomed me with grace to his home, I was glad that from his own people he had respect unmingled with mockery. We sat in his house and talked. Then he asked, 'You come here from Kiniwata?

'Yes. They say there's nothing I might want that you can't help me get.'

He smiled gently 'My wife is from Kiniwata.'

'Yes, I know.'

'They speak of her?

'A little.'

'What do they say?

'Why, just ... ' The question caught me off balance. 'They told me you were married at festival time.'

'Nothing more?' The curve of his eyebrow told me he knew there had to be more.

'They also say the marriage settlement was eight cows.' I paused. 'They wonder why.'

'They ask that?' his eyes lighted with pleasure. 'Everyone in Kiniwata knows about the eight cows?'

I nodded.

'And in Nurabandi everyone knows it, too.' His chest expanded with satisfaction. 'Always and for ever, when they speak of marriage settlement, it will be remembered that Johnny Lingo paid eight cows for Sarita.'

So that's it, I thought: vanity.

And then I saw her. I watched her enter the room to place flowers on the table. She stood still a moment to smile at the young man beside me. Then she went swiftly out again. She was the most beautiful woman I had ever seen. The lift of her shoulders, the tilt of her chin, the sparkle of her eyes all spelt a pride to which no one could deny her the right.

I turned back to Johnny Lingo and found him looking at me.

'You admire her?' he murmured.

'She . . . she's glorious. But she is not Sarita from Kiniwata,' I said.

'There's only one Sarita. Perhaps she does not look the way they say she looked in Kiniwata.'

'She doesn't. I heard she was plain. They all make fun of you because you let yourself be cheated by Sam Karoo.'

'You think eight cows were too many?' A smile slid over his lips.

'No. But how can she be so different?'

'Do you ever think', he asked, 'what it must mean to a woman to know that her husband has settled on the lowest price for which she can be bought? And then later, when the women talk, they boast of what their husbands paid for them. One says four cows, another maybe six. How does she feel, the woman who was sold for one or two? This could not happen to my Sarita.'

'Then you did this just to make your wife happy?

'I wanted Sarita to be happy, yes. But I wanted more than that. You say she is different. This is true. Many things can change a woman. Things that happen inside, things that happen outside. But the thing that matters most is what she thinks about herself. In Kiniwata, Sarita believed she was worth nothing. Now she knows she is worth more than any other woman in the islands.'

'Then you wanted . . . '

'I wanted to marry Sarita. I loved her and no other woman.'

'But . . . ' I was close to understanding.

'But', he finished softly, I wanted an eight-cow wife.'

Taken from LOVING AGAINST THE ODDS
by Rob Parsons
Copyright © 1994 The Salt Trust
Used by permission of the author

ISBN: 0-340-70983-9

BROTHER YUN
with PAUL HATTAWAY

The Heavenly Man is the dramatic story of how God took a young, half-starved boy from a poor village in China and used him to preach the gospel despite horrific opposition.

Brother Yun is one of China's house church leaders, a man who despite his relative youth has suffered prolonged torture and imprisonment for his faith. His account challenges any complacency about the situation in China, where international economic investment ignores the brutal fact that religious persecution is still a daily reality for millions. Instead of focusing on the many experiences of suffering, Yun emphasizes the character of Jesus.

Be Still and Know That I Am God

by Brother Yun with Paul Hattaway

> Because of my chains, most of the brothers in the Lord have been encouraged to speak the word of God more courageously and fearlessly. (Phil. 1:14)

I thank God for his grace and calling to me. What great power he has for those who believe in him! Despite the terrible season of persecution that was raging across China, Deling and I prepared to travel north. Together we sang a song based on the Apostle Paul's courageous declaration in Acts 20:22-24:

> And now, compelled by the Spirit, I am going to Jerusalem, not knowing what will happen to me there. I only know that in every city the Holy Spirit warns me that prison and hardships are facing me. However, I consider my life worth nothing to me, if only I may finish the race and complete the task the Lord Jesus has given me – the task of testifying to the gospel of God's grace.

We continued meeting with believers, encouraging them and seeking the Lord for guidance. During one prayer time a servant of the Lord suddenly spoke a prophecy to us: 'This time, when you and your wife go north, you will encounter danger. But no matter what happens, the Lord will be with you.'

The next morning, before the sun rose, Deling and I took the bus towards Wuyang County in the north. We passed through many bus stations displaying posters with my name and picture, announcing that I was a dangerous criminal, a counter-revolutionary. The posters accused me of being the leader of an anti-government organisation that stirred people up against state religious policies.

At one town we had to change our bus. I was wearing sunglasses to hide my eyes. Many people at the station had seen my picture and we overheard them discussing it. One man said, 'The person who helps catch this fugitive will receive a great reward from the government.'

My wife and I had an unspoken joy inside because we knew the Lord was our refuge. We felt so honoured to be wanted criminals as we walked hand-in-hand together for Jesus. It's a great honour to be humiliated for the name of the Lord.

We found the Christians in Henan were totally different from those in Hubei. They were all willing to risk their lives for us and to welcome us 'criminals' to their homes. The more tense the situation, the more they earnestly desired to show their love and respect to God's servants.

Onward we marched. A meeting was arranged at a certain village. We were led by the Holy Spirit to sing a powerful song called Martyrs for the Lord:

From the time the church was birthed on the day of Pentecost
The followers of the Lord have willingly sacrificed themselves
Tens of thousands have died that the gospel might prosper
As such they have obtained the crown of life.

Chorus:
To be a martyr for the Lord, to be a martyr for the Lord
I am willing to die gloriously for the Lord.

Those apostles who loved the Lord to the end
Willingly followed the Lord down the path of suffering
John was exiled to the lonely isle of Patmos
Stephen was stoned to death by an angry crowd.

Matthew was stabbed to death in Persia by a mob
Mark died as horses pulled his two legs apart
Doctor Luke was cruelly hanged
Peter, Philip and Simon were crucified on a cross.

Bartholomew was skinned alive by the heathen
Thomas died in India as five horses pulled his
    body apart
The apostle James was beheaded by King Herod
Little James was cut in half by a sharp saw.

James the brother of the Lord was stoned to death
Judas was tied to a pillar and shot by arrows
Matthias had his head cut off in Jerusalem
Paul was a martyr under Emperor Nero.

I am willing to take up the cross and go forward
To follow the apostles down the road of sacrifice
That tens of thousands of precious souls can be
    saved
I am willing to leave all and be a martyr for the
    Lord.

When we finished singing the whole meeting place was shaken. There was a great sound of weeping. I stood up to speak about suffering for the Lord. The Holy Spirit fell upon us and we earnestly interceded for our nation. We re-dedicated ourselves to fight for the Lord.

After the meeting Brother Zhen, a humble and faithful brother, knelt down in the courtyard after everyone else had gone to sleep, and continued to pray for our nation. The Holy Spirit clearly told him, 'Within three days there are people among you who will be bound and beaten for me. Some will even lay down their lives for me.'

After he told me this I felt the Lord was speaking to me personally. I whispered a prayer, 'Oh Father, I'm willing to suffer for your Name.'

My wife and I prayed together and we felt she needed to return home to comfort the families of our many workers who had been imprisoned. I waved goodbye to her as the local believers took her to the bus station.

For all three days of our meeting the snow kept falling. Some of the older homes in the village collapsed from the weight of the snow on their roofs. The whole village was blanketed with ice and snow, but everyone in the meeting was on fire for the Lord.

At midnight on the third day, 17 December 1983, the meeting concluded. The hosts had prepared warm water to wash everyone's feet. I washed my co-workers' feet with my tears. Then they urged me to sit down. They took off my socks and washed my feet with their tears, before gently putting my shoes back on again. Our meeting was in a place called 'The Village of Love'. How true it had turned out to be!

We split up to go to the homes of different believers to rest. Before we left, Brother Zhang took off his big winter scarf and gave it to me.

* * *

Just after we left the meeting place about a dozen men carrying flashlights confronted us at the outskirts of the village. They shouted, 'Who are you? What is your business here?' Our co-workers knew something was wrong so they turned around and ran. I also turned to run but it was too late.

One man, wielding an electric baton, ran to me and shocked me with hundreds of volts of electricity. I was immediately thrown backwards into the snow. Excruciating pain surged through my entire body.

They kicked me with their steel-capped boots and struck me with their pistol handles. Another four brothers were arrested with me. At that moment I heard a gentle voice from above that simply said two words to me, 'I know!'

I realised this was the familiar voice of my Lord Jesus, who many centuries before had told the persecuted believers in Smyrna:

I know your afflictions and your poverty – yet you are rich! I know the slander of those who say they are Jews and are not, but are a synagogue of Satan. Do not be afraid of what you are about to suffer. I tell you, the devil will put some of you in prison to test you, and you will suffer persecution for ten days. Be faithful, even to the point of death, and I will give you the crown of life. (Rev. 2:9-10)

My Lord knew what I was going through and he knew everything I would have to endure. I was greatly encouraged!

Brother Zhen's prophecy came into my mind, and all the pain left me. One officer demanded, 'What is your name? Where are you from? How many workers do you have? Where are they? Speak now! Tell the truth!' He leaned forward and spoke more threateningly than before, 'Tell me the truth. If you lie, I'll skin you alive!'

Suddenly I felt tense inside as I realised many brothers and sisters still in the meeting place were in danger of being found. The only thought I had in my mind was how I could raise an alarm so they would know trouble was at their door.

The Holy Spirit immediately reminded me of the story when King David feigned insanity when he met Abimelech. I shouted in a loud voice, 'I am a heavenly man! I live in Gospel village! People call me Morning Star! My father's name is Abundant Blessing! My mother's name is Faith, Hope, Love!'

The officers kicked me violently then dragged me to my feet. They shouted, 'What nonsense are you shouting? We asked you where you're from and who your co-workers are!'

At that moment I was facing the East. I told them, 'They're in that village over there.' I shouted again with a loud voice, 'I've been caught by the Security Police!'

The officers shoved me and ordered me to take them to find my co-workers. 'Take us. If you're lying we'll skin you alive!' they grimly threatened.

I walked ahead of them and shouted in a loud voice, 'I've been arrested by the Security Police! I don't know where the meetings took place because I'm a heavenly man! I'm not from this earth!'

I shouted louder and louder, hoping my co-workers would hear my voice and escape before they too were arrested. From that day to now, completely unknown to me at the time, I was given the nickname 'the heavenly man' by believers in China. As you can see, I didn't ask for this name, for I'm just a weak human vessel, but this is how I came to be known by this nick-name.

Instead of fleeing when they heard my shouting, many of the brothers and sisters came out to see what was going on! They were more concerned for me than for their own safety.

I led the officers through the snow, towards the village to the east. They grabbed me and demanded, 'Quickly, tell us which house! Take us in!'

I pretended to be confused and shouted, 'Oh, it's not this village. I'm mistaken! My co-workers are in another village!'

They threw me to the ground, beating and kicking me. Again the baton was used to electrocute me. I would surely have died if the Lord had not protected me.

Some brothers and sisters were silently following us at a distance. When they saw the punishment I was given they were filled with grief and started to pray. The officers noticed them.

I didn't want to place the believers at risk so I shouted again, 'I'm a heavenly man. I don't know where the meeting was. I don't know any of you who are following us. The heavenly man will never become a Judas! I only know the Master from heaven!'

The brothers and sisters realised I was warning them.

They turned around and fled. The officers were furious because I had tricked them. The four co-workers and I were pushed into the back of a tractor that had been brought to transport us to Wuyang City. We were tied together with one rope like cattle going to slaughter. Standing in the back of the tractor, I sang in a loud voice:

First comes blood, then the anointing oil
First we must be clean then we receive blessing from the Lord
First we must experience Calvary, then will come Pentecost.
Cross, cross, forever my glory

His blood has washed my sins away
Only through the blood of Jesus.

The five of us were placed in a prison cell inside
the police station. The temperature was well
below freezing. There was no heating at all, and
they had taken my coat and thrown it in the
snow. We shivered and our limbs turned blue.
We almost fell unconscious. Our frozen handcuffs cut like knives into our swollen wrists.

I used the handcuffs to knock on the door
and the iron windows. As I looked around I
saw a broken wooden box in the corner of the
cell. Inside was an old drum. I beat the drum
with my handcuffs and made a loud noise. At
the top of my voice I sang Psalm 150:

Praise the Lord.

Praise God in his sanctuary;
praise him in his mighty heavens.
Praise him for his acts of power;
praise him for his surpassing greatness.
Praise him with the sounding of the trumpet,
praise him with the harp and lyre,
praise him with tambourine and dancing,
praise him with the strings and flute,
praise him with the clash of cymbals,
praise him with resounding cymbals.
Let everything that has breath praise the Lord.
Praise the Lord.

The more I sang the more I was filled with joy. I stood up and praised the Lord. Gradually my frozen hands and feet regained feeling and I wasn't cold any more. The four brothers knelt down on the floor and earnestly prayed for China. The piercing wind whistled loudly outside, but inside our cell weeping and the groans of intercessory prayers were heard.

The guards were greatly incensed by my drumming and singing but didn't want to get out of their warm beds to stop me. The five of us encouraged and strengthened one another throughout the night. Just like Shadrach, Meshach and Abednego, we learned that where the Spirit of the Lord is, there is liberty, whether in a freezing prison cell or a fiery furnace. Hallelujah!

The next morning the guards opened the cell door and took us out into the yard. There was a thick layer of snow on the ground. They released the handcuffs from my four brothers. They told them, 'You must clear all the snow in the yard. But this crazy "heavenly man" will not have his handcuffs removed. Last night he created an uproar and kept us awake with his singing and drumming.'

The chief guard waved his electric baton in front of my face and said, 'Now is the time for you to wake up!' He ordered me to kneel down before him. I loudly protested, 'I will not kneel down before you. I will only kneel down before my God!'

He arrogantly stated, 'I am your Lord! I am your God! If you kneel down before me I can release you immediately.'

I spoke angrily to him, 'In the name of Jesus, you are not my God! You are just an earthly officer. My Lord is in heaven. I am a heavenly man.'

He turned on the power switch on his baton and snarled, 'If you are a heavenly man then you won't be afraid of this electric baton. Come! Use your hands to take hold of it!'

Several guards grabbed my arms and forced me to stretch out my hand. In an instant I was stung with hundreds of volts of electric current, like the sting of a scorpion or as if a thousand arrows had pierced my heart. Feeling I was about to pass out, I cried out, 'Lord, have mercy on me!' Immediately the electric baton malfunctioned! They couldn't get it to work!

I opened my eyes and stared at the guard who'd dared to call himself 'God'. He was terrified. Despite the temperature, he was sweating! He turned and ran away as fast as he could!

The four brothers had witnessed this event and when they saw the guards force my hand on the baton they prayed God would have mercy on me.

The next morning the five of us were shoved into a van. They took us to the prison in Wuyang.

When I entered the prison yard on the way to the cell I knew there must be many Christian brothers inside that prison because of the wave of persecution against the church. In a bid to encourage them I shouted out, 'A heavenly man has been sent to prison, I'm not like Judas! I will not betray the Lord!' After we arrived the guard locked me in the same cell as Brother Zhen and ten other men.

Some minutes later I was in my cell when I heard the prison gate open. Some more believers were being brought in. The guard on the gate asked one Christian, 'Are you a heavenly man, or are you an earthly man?'

The brother said, 'I don't know what you're talking about.' The guards wanted to know which of the Christians were like the heavenly man they had just brought in, and which were not.

This brother finally answered, 'I'm a man from the earth, not a heavenly man.'

The guard said, 'Because you're just an earthly man, tonight I will put you in the cell of a heavenly man.'

When he entered the cell I was kneeling down in prayer. I stared at him with great intensity. My spirit was so angry because he'd denied being a believer in order to make it easy on himself.

With great fervency I shouted, 'You should say No! No! No! to the devil!' I stood up and continued to shout, 'You must say No! No! No! to the devil!'

While he watched, I used my right forefinger to trace the word 'No!' on the cement wall. I pressed my finger against the rough wall so hard that it became numb and started to bleed.

With the blood from my own finger I wrote this sentence on the wall: 'No! No! No! Don't be afraid! Don't trust in man, trust only in Jesus.'

When this brother saw these words written with my own blood he felt great shame and conviction for compromising his testimony. He bowed his head and wept tears of repentance. After his release from prison he became a leader of the church in his locality.

Several old Christian women living nearby heard of our arrest. In the night they trudged through the snow to bring us their best blankets and coats. One of the old sisters even hobbled through the snow on her crutches; such was her love for the family of God!

When they arrived at the prison they told the guard they had brought these gifts for the heavenly people. The guard asked, 'For whom?'

They replied, 'For the heavenly people.'

I was staying in the cell closest to the prison office, so I could hear all of this. My heart was filled with thanksgiving when I heard of their love. I cried out, 'I am a heavenly man!' so that those dear sisters could hear my voice.

The next morning the guards had exchanged the old sisters' gifts. They threw a tattered blanket into my cell and kept the good blankets and clothes for themselves. The women had also brought me a new pair of boots, but a guard stole them for himself. The blanket I received was old and ragged, but those sisters' love gave me great faith and courage.

* * *

There were dozens of Christians in that prison, and we all endured terrible beatings and torture for the Lord. God granted us special patience and wisdom in dealing with our persecutors.

The prison authorities liked to entice some of the rough prisoners to beat up other prisoners. They offered to make their sentences lighter and bribed them with promises of better meals if they agreed to do their dirty work for them. At mealtimes we were served a tiny bowl of mouldy, mashed sweet potato paste mixed with radish. Once a week we were given a *mantou* – a small steamed bread bun. All of the prisoners were nearly starving, so this was a real treat.

One evening after I received my precious *mantou* I knelt down, closed my eyes, and gave thanks to the Lord with the *mantou* in my upraised hand. While my eyes were still closed one of the other prisoners came and snatched my bun from me. One of the guards saw the man take my *mantou* and hide it in his shirt-pocket. The guards beat him mercilessly and ordered the other prisoners to beat him too. They then forced him to kneel down inside the urinal, smearing his head with human waste.

Like brute savages they held the man's head in the urinal until he nearly drowned.

I felt so guilty! I wept loudly and uncontrollably because of what had happened to my fellow prisoner. I cried out to the Lord, 'O God, have mercy on me! Have mercy on me! Please forgive me!'

The next morning the guards took me out from the cell and practised martial arts on my body. They kicked and punched me to the ground and ordered several other prisoners to stamp on my chest and private parts. Blood gushed from my mouth. I was dizzy and in great pain. I was sure I was going to die.

Up until that time Brother Zhen and I – though we shared the same cell – pretended we didn't know each other. If the prison authorities knew two Christians were encouraging each other they would be furious. But when Brother Zhen saw what had happened to me in the yard, he rushed over to me, cradled my body in his arms, and cried, 'Heavenly man, my dear brother!' He used his sleeves to wipe the blood from my nose and mouth.

Brother Zhen served me like an angel. He always encouraged me with words of hope from the Scriptures. All the other prisoners and guards sensed he had a kind and merciful spirit so they liked him.

A few days later the Public Security Bureau sent a car to collect him and take him back to his home town for sentencing. They shouted, 'Zhen, get ready. It's time for you to leave.' Brother Zhen hated to leave me. We wept and knelt in prayer together on the floor.

'Leave in peace,' I told him.

This man of God was taken away from our prison and from our lives.

Although Brother Zhen had left, his teaching remained. Some of the prisoners began to say to each other, 'We need to believe in Jesus.' As a result, those criminals no longer treated me cruelly.

One young prisoner was an unbeliever, though his mother was a Christian. He stayed in my cell for a few days and found I wasn't mad like the guards had told him I was. He said to the other prisoners, 'Yun is not crazy. He's a man who has paid a great price for his faith in God.'

He took off his coat and gave it to me out of love and compassion. The next day the young man was released from the cell and given a job in the kitchen. A little while later he was allowed to go home and he became a committed disciple of Jesus Christ.

During those days in prison I was interrogated many times. They sensed that they had caught a 'big fish' but couldn't find out my true identity. They used every technique they knew to try to find out where I came from, so that they could go after my co-workers. I foiled their plans by refusing to answer their questions. I could never implicate the brothers and sisters in my home church.

Because I wouldn't reveal my identity, the authorities in Wuyang County sent a letter to every other county in Henan, asking them to come and see if I was from their area. Several PSB officers from other counties came and left disappointed that I wasn't who they thought I was. The prison telephoned all over the province trying to identify me.

Finally, more than five weeks after my arrest, I was identified. At around eight thirty a.m. on the morning of 25 January 1984, PSB officers from Nanyang County came and immediately recognised me. They were overjoyed. They told me, 'You're good at fooling the police here with your feigned insanity, but you don't fool us! Even if you lost your skin we'd still be able to recognise you. You've escaped from us many times and made us look stupid, but you won't escape this time!'

They slapped me and handcuffed me behind my back. They said, 'Let's go! We're taking you back to Nanyang and will deal with you when we get there.'

The Nanyang officers thanked the local PSB for taking care of me and threw me into the back of their van. They handcuffed me to a steel rail above my head that ran down the centre of the van. After closing the doors they beat me with their fists and with batons, severely wounding me.

As they drove throughout the day on the bumpy roads my handcuffs cut into my wrists so that blood splattered everywhere, covering the walls of the van. The handcuffs cut so deep that my wrist bones were exposed. I was in such agony I could hardly breathe. I was about to fall unconscious because of the pain and loss of blood.

I cried out to the Lord and said, 'Jesus, I can no longer endure. Why are you allowing me to be tortured like this? Please receive my spirit now.'

The guards travelling in the back of the van switched on an electric baton when they heard me praying and jolted me with shocks. The pain was too severe for me and I felt my heart and my brain were going to literally explode from my body. Again I cried to the Lord, 'God, have mercy on me. Please receive my spirit now.'

The word of the Lord came to me clearly. 'The reason you suffer is so you can partake in the fellowship of my suffering. Be still and know that I am God. I will be exalted among the nations. I will be exalted in the earth.'

In my proud heart I'd been thinking that I was important to the church, that they needed me to lead them. Now, I vividly understood that he is God and I am but a feeble man. I realised that God didn't need me at all, and that if he ever chose to use me again it would be nothing more than a great privilege.

Suddenly the fear and pain left me.

* * *

The police van finally entered the streets of Nanyang, my home town. They slowed down. I could see through the windows that posters had been plastered on every wall along both sides of the street, announcing, 'Celebrate and warmly congratulate the Public Security Bureau! The Christian counter-revolutionary Yun, who has clothed his criminal activities in the cloak of religion, has been apprehended!' 'The arrest of the counter-revolutionary Yun is good news for the people of Nanyang!' 'Down with the reactionary Yun and his fellow workers! Resolutely strike down all illegal Christian meetings led by Yun!'

The guards turned their siren on so they could boast to the people of their great achievement in catching me. The news of my arrest spread quickly and people rushed after the van to see me.

But I was no longer afraid. The Lord had already told me:

Do not be afraid of what you are about to suffer. I tell you, the devil will put some of you in prison to test you ...Be faithful, even to the point of death, and I will give you the crown of life. (Rev. 2:10)

From THE HEAVENLY MAN by Brother Yun
with Paul Hattaway
Copyright © Brother Yun and
Paul Hattaway 2002
Used by permission of Monarch Books
Concorde House, Grenville Place
Mill Hill, London, NW7 3SA

ISBN: 1-85424-597-X

PHILIP YANCEY

Philip Yancey is one of the most popular and acclaimed religious writers of our day. His searching and refreshingly honest books, including *What's So Amazing About Grace?* and *The Jesus I Never Knew*, have encouraged and inspired millions of people around the world.

Detours to Happiness:
Dr Paul Brand

by Philip Yancey

I spent the last four years of the 1960s as a college student. Everything in America seemed to be cracking apart then: the Vietnam war chiselled away at our national ideals, revelations about abuse of the environment challenged the industrial ethic that had built our country, and the youth counterculture exposed the hollow materialism of business and the media. The issues have since become familiar, even hackneyed, but to those of us who were forming a view of the world then, the 1960s left a profound and permanent imprint.

I recall my emotions in the subsequent years as being primarily anger, loneliness and despair. I saw bright and talented friends give up on society and seek a new path through LSD and mescaline. Others never came back from the jungles of Vietnam. I plodded through bleak existentialist novels as well as non-fiction accounts of the Holocaust and the Soviet Gulag. Looking at the church through such jaundiced eyes, I saw mainly its hypocrisy and its irrelevance to the world outside. Although people like G. K. Chesterton had led me back to God, I was still having difficulty distinguishing God from church and cultivating a stable personal faith. Questions swirled. Even while editing a Christian magazine I wrote books with titles like *Where is God when it Hurts?*, *Unhappy Secrets of the Christian Life* and *Disappointment with God*, outward projections of my own struggles with faith.

I now see that my writing partnership with Dr Paul Brand helped me weather that volatile period. I spent hundreds of hours interrogating him on global issues, life and God. On trips to India and England I tracked his life, interviewing former patients and colleagues. (Operating room scrub nurses, I found, have the keenest insight into a surgeon's character.) Proud owner of one of the first 'laptop' computers, a fourteen-pound monstrosity, I interviewed Brand himself on the go, keeping my fingers on the keyboard so that I could continue typing even as our jeep bounced along the rutted roads of rural India, or as we sat in a gently rocking London Underground carriage.

I first learned about Dr Brand while writing *Where is God when it Hurts?* As I was holed up in libraries reading books on the problem of pain, my wife, while cleaning out the cupboards of a medical-supply house, came across an intriguing

essay he had written on 'The Gift of Pain'. Brand's
approach, implied by the title itself, had about it
the paradoxical quality that had so drawn me to
Chesterton. He had a different conception of
pleasure and pain than any I had encountered. I
had interviewed scores of people who wanted
desperately to get rid of pain; Brand told of
spending several million dollars trying to create a
pain system for his patients.

As I enquired further, and talked to people
who knew Brand personally, I became so capti-
vated that I called him out of the blue from
Chicago and asked for an interview. 'Well, they
keep me pretty busy here,' he replied, a bit non-
plussed. 'But I'm sure we could carve out some
time in between meetings and clinics. Come
ahead if you like.'

We met on the grounds of the only leprosarium in the continental United States. After flying
to New Orleans and renting a car, I drove for
two hours along the banks of the Mississippi
river past crumbling old plantations, crawfish
cafes and gleaming new petrochemical factories. My eyes were burning from the factories'
pollutants by the time I found the road that led
to the backwater town of Carville, and then a
smaller road that ended at the National
Hansen's Disease Hospital and Research Center.

The Louisiana authorities that founded the
hospital situated it well away from population
centres. (Due to myths about the disease,

'not-in-my-back-yard' sentiments tend to reach a feverish pitch when a leprosarium is proposed.) Laid out in sprawling, colonial style under massive oak trees, Carville resembled a movie set of a Philippine plantation. I could see patients on crutches and in wheelchairs moving slowly along the double-decker arched walkways that connected the major buildings. Surrounding the hospital on three sides were a golf course and baseball diamonds, a vegetable garden and an enclave of staff housing. To the west lay the mighty Mississippi, hidden from view by a twenty-foot levee. I opened the car door and stepped into a fog of delta humidity.

I knew of Brand's stature in the world medical community in advance of my visit: the offers to head up major medical centres in England and the United States; the distinguished lectureships all over the world; the hand-surgery procedures named in his honour; the prestigious Albert Lasker Award; his appointment as Commander of the Order of the British Empire by Queen Elizabeth II; his selection as the only Westerner to serve on the Mahatma Gandhi Foundation. Yet I awaited our interview in a cubbyhole of an office hardly suggestive of such renown. Stacks of medical journals, photographic slides and unanswered correspondence covered every square inch of an ugly government-green metal desk. An antique window air-conditioner throbbed at the decibel level of an unsilenced motorcycle.

Finally, a slight man of less-than-average height and stiff posture entered the room. He had greying hair, bushy eyebrows and a face that creased deeply when he smiled. In a British accent – a striking contrast to the bayou tones heard in hospital corridors – he apologised for the flecks of blood on his lab coat, explaining that he had just been dissecting armadillos, the only non-human species known to harbour leprosy bacilli.

That first visit lasted a week. I accompanied Brand on hospital rounds, hugging corridor walls to avoid the whirring electric wheelchairs and bicycles customised with sidecars. I sat in the examination room as he studied the inflamed, ulcerated feet and hands of patients, whom he quizzed like a detective in an effort to determine the injuries' cause. We grabbed bits of conversation in his office, sometimes interrupted by a call from overseas: a surgeon in Venezuela or India or Turkey shouting through the static to ask advice on a difficult procedure.

At night in their wooden bungalow on the hospital grounds, I would share a rice-and-curry meal with Brand and his wife, Margaret, a respected ophthalmologist. Then Paul Brand would prop up his bare feet (a trademark with him) and I would turn on the tape recorder for discussions that ranged from leprology and theology to world hunger and soil conservation. Every topic I brought up he had thought about in some depth, and his travel gave him a truly global perspective: he had spent a third of his life in England, a third in India, and now almost a third in the United States. During breaks he taught me such things as how to select a ripe fig (watch the ones butterflies light on several times, testing), how to stroke skin with a stiff hairbrush to stimulate nerve cells and relieve pain, how to make a mango milkshake.

We made an odd couple, Dr Brand and I. I was a young punk in my mid-twenties with bushy Art Garfunkel-style hair; Brand was a dignified, silver-haired surgeon characterised by proper British reserve. In my role as a journalist I had interviewed many subjects: actors and musicians, politicians, successful business executives, Olympic and professional athletes, Nobel laureates and Pulitzer Prize winners. Something attracted me to Brand at deeper level than I had felt with any other interview subject. For perhaps the first time, I encountered genuine humility.

Brand was still adjusting to life in the United States. He worried about the impact of television and the popular music culture on his children. Everyday luxuries made him nervous, and he longed for the simple life close to the soil in village India. When I talked him into going to a restaurant in the evening, he could hardly stand watching the waste of food scraped uneaten off diners' plates. He knew presidents, kings and many famous people, but he rarely mentioned them, preferring instead to reminisce about individual leprosy patients. He talked openly about his failures, and always tried to deflect credit for his successes to his associates. Every day he rose early to study the Bible and to pray. Humility and gratitude flowed from him naturally, and in our time together I sensed desperate lack of these qualities in myself.

Most speakers and writers I knew were hitting the circuit packaging and repackaging the same thoughts in different books and giving the same speeches to different crowds. Meanwhile Paul Brand, who had more intellectual and spiritual depth than anyone I had ever met, gave many of his speeches to a handful of leprosy patients in the hospital's Protestant chapel. At the Brands' insistence, I attended the Wednesday evening prayer service during my week at Carville. If I recall correctly, there were five of us in the choir and eight in the audience. Margaret Brand had drafted me into the choir, pleading, 'We haven't had a male voice in ever so long. Paul is giving the sermon, so he's not available. You simply must sing with us.' She brushed aside my mild protests. 'Don't be silly. Half the people who attend are deaf because of a reaction to a drug we use in treating leprosy. But a guest chorister would be such a treat – they'll enjoy just watching you.' To that motley crew, Brand proceeded to deliver an address worthy of Westminster Abbey. Obviously, he had spent hours meditating and praying over that one sermon. It mattered not that we were a tiny cluster of half-deaf nobodies in a sleepy bayou chapel. He spoke as an act of worship, as one who truly believed that God shows up when two or three are gathered together in God's name.

Later that week Brand admitted to me, somewhat shyly, that he had once tried writing a book. Some years before, when he had delivered a series of talks to a medical school in Vellore, India, other faculty members encouraged him to write them down for publication. He made the effort, but the material filled only ninety pages, not enough for a book. Twenty years had passed, and he had not touched the manuscript since. I persuaded him to dig through cupboards and bureau drawers until he located the badly smudged third carbon copy of those chapel talks, and that night I sat up long past midnight reading his remarkable meditations on the human body. I was staying in the hospital's antebellum guestroom, and a ceiling fan periodically scattered the onionskin pages around the room. I kept gathering them up and re-sorting them, though, for I knew I had struck gold. The next day I asked Brand if we could collaborate, and those ninety pages eventually became two full-length books.

Some time later we worked on a third volume, *The Gift of Pain*. In all I have spent almost ten years following the threads of Dr Brand's life. I have often felt like James Boswell, who tailed the great man Samuel Johnson and loyally recorded every morsel of wisdom that fell from his lips. Brand's daughter Pauline once thanked me for bringing some order to 'the happy jumble of my father's life and thoughts'. Little did she know the role her father played in bringing some order to the unhappy jumble of my own life. True friends get their measure, over time, in their effect on you. As I compare the person I was in 1975, on our first meeting, and the person I am now, I realise that seismic changes have occurred within me, with Brand responsible for many of those tremors.

Paul Brand is both a good and a great man, and I am forever grateful for the time we spent together. At a stage when I had slight confidence to write about my own fledgling faith, I had absolute confidence writing about his. My faith grew as I observed with a journalist's critical eye a person enhanced in every way by his relationship with God. I came to know him as an actual living model whom I could watch in action: at Carville with his patients; in the villages of India;

as a husband and father; as a speaker at both medical and spiritual conferences.

After retiring from medical practice, Dr Brand moved to a small cottage overlooking Puget Sound in Seattle, the only home he has ever owned. He served a few terms as President of the International Christian Medical and Dental Society, consulted with the World Health Organization, and into his eighties continued to lecture throughout the world. As the years passed, our roles inevitably reversed. He started calling me for advice on such matters as which word-processing software to use, how to organise notes and how to deal with publishers. He suffered a stroke on a trip to Turkey and a mild heart attack in London (a sympathetic reaction to his wife's more serious heart attack). For a time his speech slurred noticeably, and his ability to recall names and events faded. Our conversation moved to issues of ageing and mortality.

As I proceed through stages of life, now approaching Brand's own age at the time of our first meeting, before me I have his slight but strong figure showing me the way. Deprived of my own father in infancy, I received as an adult from Brand much that I had missed. As much as anyone, he has helped set my course in outlook, spirit and ideals. I look at the natural world, and environmental issues, largely through his eyes. From him I also have gained assurance that the Christian life I had heard in theory can actually work out in practice. It is indeed possible to live it in modern society, achieve success without forfeiting humility, serve others sacrificially, and yet emerge with joy and contentment. To this day, whenever I doubt that, I look back on my time with Paul Brand.

* * *

Is the universe a friendly place? Einstein asked. A scientist, he searched for an answer in the vast reaches of the cosmos. Anyone who has survived the wounds of a dysfunctional family or church knows the more personal side of that question. An uncle, or perhaps a priest, sexually abuses a young child; a mother flies into an alcoholic rage; a six-year-old sibling contracts leukaemia. For one who grows up in such an environment, the questions never go away. Is the world a friendly place? Can people be trusted? Can God?

I need not brood long over my own childhood to recognise these fundamental questions gnawing at my soul. In adolescence, as I read books like Sartre's *Nausea*, Camus's *The Plague* and Wiesel's *Night*, I had little reason for optimism. And then I found myself collaborating with a man who had spent much of his life among the most mistreated human beings on the planet. Unexpectedly, instead of intensifying my questions, Dr Brand pointed towards something of an answer.

Brand achieved fame in the medical world mainly through his pioneering research on the world's oldest and most feared disease. Before moving to the Carville hospital, he had directed a large medical college and hospital in Vellore, India, and founded a leprosy centre known as Karigiri. Leprosy disproportionately afflicts the poor. Left untreated, its victims can develop the facial disfigurement, blindness and loss of limbs that so frightens people, who in turn respond with abuse and mistreatment. In a place like India, people with leprosy are the outcasts of society, often doubly so as members of the Untouchable caste.

In biblical times leprosy victims kept a wide berth and shouted 'Unclean!' if anyone approached. In mediaeval times they lived outside town walls and wore warning bells. Even today in modern India, home to four million leprosy victims, a person showing signs of the disease may be kicked – literally, with a shoe – out of family and village to lead a beggar's life. Interviewing Brand's former patients, I heard stories of human cruelty almost beyond belief. If anyone has a right to bitterness or despair, it should be someone who works with these unfortunates. Instead, the single characteristic that most impressed me about Paul Brand was his bedrock sense of gratitude. For him, the universe is assuredly a friendly place.

I remember well our first conversation, for somehow I neglected to press the red 'Record' button on the cassette recorder I was using. That evening, after discovering the error, I took a ferry across the Mississippi, sat in a crawfish cafe and frantically tried to recall our conversation. I had a list of all my questions, and his answers had so impressed me that I found I could reconstruct them almost verbatim. As I dipped into the basket of shiny red crustaceans with one hand, I feverishly wrote down everything I remembered with the other, occasionally dripping butter on my notebook pages.

How could a good God allow such a blemished world to exist? Brand had responded to my complaints one by one. Disease? Did I know that of the 24,000 species of bacteria, all but a few hundred are healthful, not harmful? Plants could not produce oxygen, nor could animals digest food without the assistance of bacteria. Indeed, bacteria constitute half of all living matter. Most agents of disease, he explained, vary from these necessary organisms in only slight mutations.

What about birth defects? He launched into a description of the complex biochemistry involved in producing one healthy child. The great wonder is not that birth defects occur but that millions more do not. Could a mistake-proof world have been created so that the human genome with its billions of variables would never err in transmission? No scientist could envision such an error-free system in our world of fixed physical laws.

'I've found it helpful to try to think like the Creator,' Brand told me. 'My engineering team at Carville has done just that. For several years our team worked with the human hand, seeking ways to protect the hands of leprosy patients who can no longer feel pain. What engineering perfection we find there! I have a bookcase filled with surgical textbooks that describe operations people have devised for the injured hand: different ways to rearrange the tendons, muscles and joints, ways to replace sections of bones and mechanical joints – thousands of surgical procedures. But I know of no procedure that succeeds in improving a normal hand. For example, the best materials we use in artificial joint replacements have a coefficient of friction one fifth that of the body's joints, and these replacements only last a few years. All the techniques correct the deviants, the one hand in a hundred that is not functioning as God designed. After operating on thousands of hands, I must agree with Isaac Newton, "In the absence of any other proof, the thumb alone would convince me of God's existence.'"

I kept proposing exceptions, and Brand dealt with each. Even at its worst, he continued, our natural world shows evidence of careful design. Like a tour guide at an art museum, he excitedly described the beautiful way torn muscle filaments reconnect, 'like the teeth of interlocking combs', after an injury. 'And do you know about the ductus arteriosus? A bypass vessel, it routes blood directly to a developing foetus's extremities, instead of to the lungs. At the moment of birth, suddenly all blood must pass through the lungs to receive oxygen because now the baby is breathing air. In a flash, a flap descends like a curtain, deflecting the blood flow, and a muscle constricts the ductus arteriosus. After performing that one act, the muscle gradually dissolves and gets absorbed by the rest of the body. Without this split-second adjustment, the baby could never survive outside the womb.'

Our conversation was the first of many anatomy lessons I would get from Dr Brand. His ability to recall what he had studied in medical school thirty years before impressed me, certainly, but something else stood out: a childlike enthusiasm, an ebullient sense of wonder at God's good creation. Listening to him, my own Chestertonian sense of wonder reawakened. I had been focusing on the apparent flaws in creation; this doctor who spent all day working with those flaws had instead an attitude of appreciation, even reverence. That attitude, I would learn, traced back to a childhood spent close to nature.

* * *

A son of missionary parents in the remote hill country of India, Brand grew up in a world of tropical fruit trees and of butterflies, birds and other animals. His artistic mother tried to capture its beauty with her paints. His father, Jesse, a self-taught naturalist, saw everywhere in nature the fingerprint of the Creator. He would lead his son to a towering termite mound and explain the marvels of co-operative termite society: 'Ten thousand legs – working together as if commanded by a single brain, all frantic except the queen, big and round as a sausage, who lies oblivious, pumping out eggs.' He would point to the sandy funnel of an ant lion trap, or the nest of a weaver bird, or a swarm of bees hanging from a tree branch. Paul did his school lessons in a tree house high up in a jackfruit tree, and sometimes studied at night by the throbbing light of a firefly jar.

Education interrupted Paul Brand's paradise when he was sent to England at the age of nine. Five years later, a teenager far from family and home, he received a telegram announcing that his father had died of blackwater fever. A letter soon arrived, mailed by ship weeks before his father's death, which became for him a kind of final legacy. Jesse Brand described the hills around their home and concluded, 'God means us to delight in his world. It isn't necessary to know botany or zoology or biology in order to enjoy the manifold life of nature. Just observe. And remember. And compare. And be always looking to God with thankfulness and worship for having placed you in such a delightful corner of the universe as the planet Earth.'

Jesse Brand's son kept his advice, and keeps it to this day, whether hiking on the Olympic Peninsula or stalking birds in the swamps of Louisiana or lecturing to medical students about the wonders of the bodies they will be treating. First in the hills of India, and later through his study of the human body, he came to realise that the natural world conceals traces of God, and the God he found there was good. It was a message I needed, from a messenger I learned to trust.

Brand's career centred on perhaps the most problematic aspect of creation: the existence of pain. I was writing the book *Where is God when it Hurts?*; he invited me to consider an alternative world without pain. He insisted on pain's great value, holding up as proof the terrible results of leprosy – damaged faces, blindness, and loss of fingers, toes and limbs – all of which occur as side effects of painlessness. As a young doctor in India, Brand had made the ground-breaking medical discovery that leprosy does its damage merely by destroying nerve endings. People who lose pain sensation then damage themselves by such simple actions as gripping a splintered rake or wearing tight shoes. Pressure sores form, infection sets in, and no pain signals alert them to tend to the wounded area. I saw such damage first-hand in Brand's clinics.

'I thank God for pain,' Brand declared with the utmost sincerity. 'I cannot think of a greater gift I could give my leprosy patients.' He went on to describe the intricacies of the pain system that protects the human body: it takes firm pressure on a very sharp needle for the sole of the foot to feel pain, whereas the cornea of the eye senses one-thousandth as much pressure, calling for a blink reflex when a thin eyelash or speck of dust brushes the surface. Intestines do not sense pain from being cut or burned; dangers these internal organs do not normally confront – yet they send out the urgent pain signal of colic when distended.

'We doctors experience a rude awakening after medical school,' Brand continued. 'After studying the marvels of the human body, suddenly I was thrust into a position much like the complaint desk of a department store. Not once did a person visit my office to express appreciation for a beautifully functioning kidney or lung. They came to complain that something was not working properly. Only later did I realise that the very things they complained about were their greatest allies. Most people view pain as an enemy. Yet, as my leprosy patients prove, it forces us to pass attention to threats against our bodies. Without it, heart attacks, strokes, ruptured appendixes and stomach ulcers would all occur without any warning. Who would ever visit a doctor apart from pain's warnings?

'I noticed that the symptoms of illness my patients complained about were actually a display of bodily healing at work. Virtually every response of our bodies that we view with irritation or disgust – blister, callus, swelling, fever, sneeze, cough, vomiting and especially pain – demonstrates a reflex towards health. In all these things normally considered enemies, we can find a reason to be grateful.'

I had often puzzled over the Bible's dramatic scene when Job, the prototype of innocent sufferers, confronts God with his complaints about suffering. The speech God gave in reply has endured as one of the great nature passages in literature, a superb celebration of wildness. To the problem of pain itself, however, God gave no direct answer, only this challenge to Job: if I, as Creator, have produced such a marvellous world as this, which you can plainly observe, can you not trust me with those areas you cannot comprehend?

As I listened to Brand, I realised that I had been approaching God like a sick patient – as if the Creator were running a complaint desk. I anguished over the tragedies, diseases and injustices, all the while ignoring the many good things surrounding me in this world. Was it possible, I wondered, to retain a Chestertonian enthusiasm for the marvels of the natural world despite its apparent flaws? Like the psalmists, could I learn to praise and lament at the same time, with neither intonation drowning out the other?

Brand responded to this same dilemma with a twin spirit of gratitude and trust – gratitude for those things he could see and appreciate, and trust regarding those things he could not. I remembered Chesterton's description of an 'ordinary person who accepts the world as a gift, the proper response to which is gratitude.' To Brand's surprise, faith in God's trustworthiness deepened even as he worked among people least likely to feel gratitude, leprosy victims in India, because he saw the transformations in the lowest of the low resulting from simple compassion and a healing touch.

As I began working with Brand and following him around the world, I met many other dedicated Christians who devote their lives to healing the wounds of humanity. In India, for example, where less than three per cent of the population claims to be Christian, nearly a fifth of all medical work is performed by Christian doctors and nurses, many of them trained at Brand's old hospital in Vellore. I accompanied them on mobile visits to villages, where they treated tropical infections, set bones and performed minor surgery, often outdoors under a tamarind tree. They served Hindus, Muslims, Sikhs, Jains, Parsis and Communists alike. If you say the word 'Christian' to an Indian peasant – who may never have heard of Jesus Christ – the first image to pop into his or her mind may well be that of a hospital, or of a medical van that stops by his or her village once a month to provide free, personal care.

Watching these people serve in difficult conditions with low pay and few benefits, I saw a sharp contrast between their approach and my own. I sat at home in Chicago and wrote books demanding answers from God about the problems of this world. They volunteered for the front lines in a truly incarnational response. Like the Brands, they showed a level of personal fulfilment and even happiness that I had not found among many famous people I had interviewed.

I learned that part of the answer to my question 'Where is God when it hurts?' is a related question: 'Where is the church when it hurts?' As the Jewish theologian Abraham Heschel wrote, 'The cardinal issue, Why does the God of justice and compassion permit evil to persist? is bound up with the problem of how man should aid God so that his justice and compassion prevail.' From the gentle touch of health workers like Paul and Margaret Brand, leprosy patients in India have learned that caste is not fate and disease is not destiny, and in that same touch many first sense the tactile reality of God's own love.

* * *

Although I have great respect for Dr Brand and his service to God, I also confess relief that he is not a 'saint' out of the mould of Francis of Assisi or Mother Teresa. I needed an up-close model of someone I could relate to more naturally.

Paul Brand consulted with Mother Teresa, served on committees with Gandhi's disciples and knew some of India's traditional 'holy men'. In his own life, however, he chose the middle way of balancing off the material and the mystical, the prophetic and the pragmatic. Older acquaintances at the hospital in Vellore remember him not only for his spiritual depth and sacrificial service but also for his practical jokes, love for marmalade and mangoes, and fast driving. As I emerged from the 1960s, a decade never accused of a sense of balance, I needed an example of someone who lived a well-rounded life in the midst of modern society, not off in a monastery or ashram.

Brand has struggled with the tensions facing modern civilisation while not giving in to either side. On the one hand, he lived a counterculture lifestyle long before such a phrase entered the vocabulary. In India he insisted on receiving Indian wages, not the much higher amount usually granted foreign doctors. The Brands have always eaten simply, relying mainly on home-made breads and vegetables grown in their organic garden. Dr Brand acknowledges a few reasons for discarding clothes – unpatchable rips, for instance – but lack of stylishness is certainly not one of them. Furniture in his home and office is, to put it kindly, unpretentious. He opposes waste in all forms. Brand admits he would shed no tears personally if all advances from the industrial revolution suddenly disappeared; he prefers village life in India, close to the outdoors.

On the other hand, he has learned to use the tools made available by modern technology. Under his leadership, a hospital in the dusty town of Vellore grew into the most modern and sophisticated facility in all of southwest Asia. Later, Brand came to Carville in the United States because that research centre offered the technological support needed to benefit millions of leprosy patients world-wide. And when personal computers were introduced in the 1980s, he signed up with boyish enthusiasm for one of the first IBMs. He gratefully uses electron microscopes and thermograms and jet planes, believing that technology's tools, used wisely and not destructively, can serve the higher goal of human compassion.

My conversations with Brand have often strayed to the question of lifestyle, for his experiences in India, England and America have afforded him a unique perspective. He has lived in one of the poorest countries and two of the richest. Affluence in the West, he recognises, offers a deadly temptation. The enormous gap in wealth can widen the moat separating the West from the rest of the world, dulling us to cries of need and justice.

The lifelong tension over lifestyle traces back to Brand's childhood in India. After her husband's death from blackwater fever, Paul's mother took on the style of a saint in the traditional sense. She lived on a pittance, devoting her life to bringing physical and spiritual healing to villagers in five mountain ranges. She cared nothing for her personal appearance, to the extent of banning all mirrors from her house. She continued making hazardous journeys on her pony even after suffering concussions and fractures from falls. Although tropical diseases ravaged her own body, she gave all her energies to treating the diseases and injuries of the people around her. Sometimes 'Granny Brand' would embarrass Paul with an intemperate outburst: at an official dinner in Vellore, for example, she might ask in horror, 'How could you possibly dine on such fine food when I have people back in the hills starving to death this very night!' She died at age ninety-five, and at her funeral thousands of villagers walked for miles to honour her in the chapel her husband had built by hand.

From his parents Paul learned the enduring lesson that love can only be applied person-to-person. They left behind few lasting institutions, only their permanent imprint on thousands of lives to whom they had taught health, sanitation, farming and the Christian gospel. Single-handedly, Granny Brand rid huge areas of a guinea worm infection that had persisted for centuries. She had earned such trust that villagers followed her instructions on building stone walls around the open wells where the larvae bred; no government programme had been so effective.

Yet her son, Paul Brand, made his most lasting impact through rigid scientific disciplines. At Vellore he fought his wife, Margaret, for space in the freezer, preserving cadaver hands on which he could practise surgical techniques by lamplight. For years he puzzled over the physiology of leprosy symptoms: which cells does it attack, and why? The answer, his most important medical discovery, came during an autopsy, when he concluded that the leprosy bacillus only attacked nerve tissue. Proving that theory required more years of research, in which he had to identify the precise cause of every patient's injuries. The results of such research had a dramatic effect on the treatment of leprosy and other anaesthetic diseases world-wide. Fifteen million victims of leprosy gained hope that, with proper care, they could preserve their toes and fingers and eyesight. Later, he applied the same principles to the insensitive feet of diabetics, helping to prevent, by one estimate, 70,000 amputations annually in the United States alone.

Brand told me of a comment made by Mother Teresa as he consulted with her on a leprosy clinic she was opening in Calcutta. 'We have drugs for people with diseases like leprosy,' she said. 'But these drugs do not treat the main problem, the disease of being unwanted. That's what my sisters hope to provide.'

In one of our conversations, Brand mused on why there are Christian missions devoted exclusively to leprosy. Much of his work in India was funded by the Leprosy Mission of England, sister organisation to the American Leprosy Mission. 'I know of no Arthritis Mission or Diabetes Mission,' he said. 'The answer, I think, relates to the incredible stigma that has surrounded leprosy for so many centuries. To work with leprosy required more than a natural instinct of compassion; it required a kind of supernatural calling. People such as Father Damien, who ministered to leprosy patients in Hawaii and then contracted the disease himself, believed that human beings, no matter what their affliction, should never be cast aside. It was up to the church to care for the sick, the unwanted, the unloved.'

As I studied the history of leprosy in my writings with Brand, I got acquainted with the saintly few who, defying society's stigma, looked past the unsightly symptoms and ministered to leprosy's victims. As the disease ravaged Europe during the Middle Ages, orders of nuns devoted to Lazarus, the patron saint of leprosy, established homes for patients. These courageous women could do little but bind wounds and change dressings, but the homes themselves, called lazarettos, may have helped break the hold of the disease in Europe, by isolating leprosy patients and improving their living conditions. In the nineteenth and twentieth centuries Christian missionaries who spread across the globe established colonies for leprosy patients, and as a result most of the major scientific advances in treating leprosy came from missionaries.

The Carville hospital itself (recently closed in a government cost-saving measure) has a history typical of leprosy work world-wide. The first seven patients, chased out of New Orleans, were smuggled by authorities up the Mississippi on a coal barge, since nineteenth-century laws forbade people with leprosy from travelling on any form of public transportation. They landed at an abandoned, rundown plantation, which the state of Louisiana had quietly procured. A few slave cabins were still standing, populated mainly by rats, bats and snakes. The seven patients moved into the Louisiana Leper Home, but the state had difficulty recruiting workers for the leprosarium until finally the Daughters of Charity, an order of Catholic nuns, volunteered. These women, nicknamed 'the White Caps', did much of the initial labour. Rising two hours before daylight to pray, wearing starched white uniforms in bayou heat, the nuns drained swamps, levelled roads and repaired buildings for the new leprosarium. Their successors were still serving at Carville when I visited Brand there.

In India, a melting-pot of religions, Brand observed how other religions responded to the problem of pain. Buddhists taught a serene acceptance of suffering, an attitude that we in the hypochondriacal West could surely learn from. Hindus and Muslims often faced suffering with a spirit of fatalism: to the Hindu it results from sins of a former life, and it is the will of Allah to the Muslim. In contrast, Christianity has traditionally responded with the paradox modelled by Jesus: we must trust the goodness of God despite the suffering and injustice we see around us, and yet do all we can to relieve it during our days on earth. Paul Brand gave me a living example of that response.

* * *

In his twilight years, Dr Brand has accepted many invitations from medical schools that want him to address the dehumanisation of medicine. Today, high-tech medicine, medical insurance policies and increasing specialisation conspire to squelch the very instincts that draw many of the best students into the field. Brand expresses the guiding principle of his medical career this way: 'The most precious possession any human being has is his spirit, his will to live, his sense of dignity, his personality. Though technically we may be concerned with tendons, bones and nerve endings, we must never lose sight of the person we are treating.'

Although our conversations together cover a broad range of topics, inevitably they drift back to stories of individuals, Brand's former patients. Most often, these patients are the forgotten people, ostracised from family and village because of their illness. A medical staff can repair much of the physical damage. They can also provide that most basic human need, touch. But what can they do for the spirit of the patient, the corroded self-image? For hours at a time I have sat and listened to Brand tell me stories of these patients and their families, and the extraordinary treatment they got in the Karigiri leprosarium. I am amazed that an orthopaedic surgeon knows so much about patients he treated decades before, and more amazed at the tears that freely flow as he tells their stories. Quite obviously, they made as great an impression on him as he made on them.

It takes a few pennies a day to arrest leprosy's progress with sulfone drugs. It takes thousands of dollars, and the painstaking care of skilled professionals, to restore to wholeness a patient in whom the disease has spread unchecked. Brand began with the rigid claw-hands, experimenting with tendon and muscle transfers until he found the very best combination to restore a full range of movement. The surgeries and rehabilitation stretched over months and sometimes years. He applied similar procedures to feet, correcting the deformities caused by years of walking without a sense of pain to guide the body in distributing weight and pressure.

Restored feet and hands gave a leprosy patient the capability to earn a living, but who would hire an employee bearing the scars of the dread disease? Brand's first patients returned to him distraught, asking him to reverse the effects of surgery so that they could return to begging, a profession that exploited obvious deformities. Paul and Margaret Brand worked together to correct that cosmetic damage. They learned to remake a human nose by entering it through the space between gum and upper lip, stretching out the skin and moist lining, then building up a new nasal structure from the inside with bone transplant. They sought to prevent blindness by restoring the ability to blink. Leprosy deadens the tiny pain cells that prompt a healthy person to blink several times a minute, and eventually the dryness leads to blindness. Margaret learned to tunnel a muscle that is normally used for chewing up under the cheek and attach it to the upper eyelid. By chewing gum all day long, her patients simultaneously moved their eyelids up and down, lubricating the eyes and thus averting blindness. Finally, the Brands replaced lost eyebrows on the faces of their patients by tunnelling a piece of scalp, intact with its nerve and blood supply, under the skin of the forehead and sewing it in place above the eyes. The first patients proudly grew their new eyebrows to enormous, bushy lengths.

All this elaborate medical care went to 'nobodies', victims of leprosy who had mostly made their living from begging. Many who arrived at the hospital barely looked human. Their shoulders slumped, they cringed when other people approached, and the light had faded from their eyes. Months of compassionate treatment from the staff at Karigiri could return that light to their eyes. For years people had shrunk away from them in terror; at Karigiri nurses and doctors would hold their hands and talk to them.

Unrevolted, unafraid, the staff listened to the new patients' stories, and used the magic of human touch. A year or so later these patients, Lazarus-like, would walk out of the hospital and proudly head off to learn a trade.

As Brand reflects now, the process of following patients through the full rehabilitation cycle ultimately challenged his whole approach towards medicine. Somewhere, perhaps in medical school, doctors acquire an attitude that seems suspiciously like hubris: 'Oh, you've come just in time. Count on me. I think I'll be able to save you.' Working at Karigiri stripped away that hubris. No one could 'save' leprosy patients. The staff could arrest the disease, yes, and repair some of the damage. Eventually, however, every leprosy patient had to go back and, against overwhelming odds, attempt to build a new life. Brand began to see his chief contribution as one he had not studied in medical school: to join with his patient as a partner in the task of restoring dignity to a broken spirit. 'We are treating a person, not a disease,' he says. 'That is the true meaning of rehabilitation.'

The great societies of the West have been moving away from an underlying belief in the value of a single human soul. We tend to view history in terms of groups of people: classes, political parties, races, sociological groupings. We apply labels to each other, and explain behaviour and ascribe worth on the basis of those labels. After prolonged exposure to Dr Brand, I realised that I had been seeing large human problems in a mathematical model: percentages of Gross National Product, average annual income, mortality rate, doctors-per-thousand of population. Love, however, is not mathematical; we can never precisely calculate the greatest possible good to be applied equally to the world's poor and needy. We can only seek out one person, and then another, and then another, as objects for God's love.

I had been wrestling with issues facing humanity. Yet I had not learned to love individuals – people created in the image of God. I would not predict a leprosarium in India as the most likely place to learn about the infinite worth of human beings, but a visit there makes the lesson unavoidable.

* * *

On my last trip to India with Paul Brand, in 1990, he showed me his childhood home in the Kolli Malai mountains. Our jeep ascended a remarkable highway featuring seventy switchbacks (each one neatly labelled: 38/70, 39/70, 40/70). A motorcycle passed us, a woman passenger clinging to the back of its driver, her sari flowing out behind her like a flag. The hairpin curves stirred Brand's memories. 'There was no highway then,' he said. 'As a child I rode in a canvas contraption slung from porters' shoulders on bamboo poles. When I grew old enough to walk, I used to totter along at eye level with the porters' legs. I watched for the tiny leeches that would leap from the shrub, fasten to those legs, and swell with blood.'

On this trip, however, we worried more about overheating the radiator than about leeches. Finally the road levelled off and wound across a high plateau, giving us spectacular views of the verdant green rice paddies below and the pale, curvy lines across the horizon that marked other mountain ranges in the distance. Then the asphalt ended and the road dived down into a small valley. Gravel gave way to dirt, then to a pair of ruts running along a line of eucalyptus trees. We followed the ruts for half an hour without seeing a single person, and I began to wonder if our driver had lost his way.

Suddenly the jeep crested a small hill and an amazing sight met us. A hundred and fifty people were waiting alongside the road – and had been waiting, we soon learned, for four hours. They surrounded our car, greeting us in the traditional Indian fashion, palms held together, head bowed. Women, colourful as tropical birds in their bright silk saris, draped floral leis around our necks and led us to a feast spread on banana leaves. After the meal everyone crowded into the mud-walled chapel built by Paul Brand's father and treated us to an hour-long programme of hymns, tributes and ceremonial dances.

I remember one speech especially, by a woman who spoke of Paul's mother. 'The hill tribes didn't practise abortion,' she said. 'They disposed of unwanted children by leaving them beside the road. Granny Brand would take in these children, nurse them back to health, rear them, and try to educate them. I was one of the unwanted ones, left to die. There were several dozen of us, but she treated it more like an adoption centre than an orphanage. We called her Mother of the Hills. When I did well in studies, she paid for me to go off to a proper school, and eventually I earned a Master's degree. I now teach nursing at the University of Madras, and I came several hundred miles today to honour the Brands for what they did for me and many others.'

After he had made a little speech and wiped away the tears, Dr Brand led me outdoors to see the legacy his parents had left. He pointed out the hand-sawn wooden house his father had built, capping the stilts with upside-down frying pans to foil the termites. A clinic was still functioning, along with a school – his parents founded nine in the hills – and carpentry shop. Citrus orchards spread out across the hills, one of Granny Brand's pet agricultural projects. Her husband, Jesse, had set up half a dozen farms for mulberry trees, bananas, sugar cane, coffee and tapioca. Paul kept remarking on how tall the jacaranda trees had grown since his father planted them seven decades before. Their fallen lavender blossoms carpeted the ground. When time came to leave, he took me to the site of his parents' graves, just down the slope from the bungalow where he grew up. 'Their bodies lie here, but their spirit lives on,' he said. 'Just look around you.'

Paul chose a different course in life from his general-missionary parents, becoming an orthopaedic surgeon. In order to see his legacy, I visited his former patients. One man, Namo, had a twenty-year-old photo of Brand on his wall, captioned 'May the Spirit that is in him live in me.' When Namo told me his story, I could easily understand the affection he feels for his former surgeon.

As a youth Namo had to leave university in the middle of his final year; telltale patches of leprosy had appeared on his skin, and his hand was retracting into a claw position. Rejected by his school, his village and finally his family, Namo made his way to the leprosarium in southern India where a young doctor was trying out some experimental hand surgery techniques. There were four million people with leprosy in India, and fifteen million world-wide, but Brand was the only orthopaedic surgeon attempting to treat their deformities.

Namo recalled that dark day: 'I was so angry at my condition I could hardly speak. Stuttering, I told Dr Brand my hands were now useless to me. Soon my feet would be too. For all I cared, he could cut them off.' Namo made a slashing motion with one hand across his other wrist. 'Anyway, he could do anything he wanted if he thought he might learn something.'

Fortunately, Namo was wrong about his prognosis. Drugs halted the spread of the disease. And after undergoing a painstaking series of surgical procedures over a five-year period, he regained the use of his hands and feet. He took training in physiotherapy, began working with other leprosy patients, and went on to become Chief of Physical Therapy at the All-India Institute.

Later that day I visited Sadan, another former patient. He looked like a miniature version of Gandhi: skinny, balding, with thick spectacles, perched cross-legged on the edge of a bed. The door to his modest apartment was open, and small birds flew in and out. A mangy dog lounged on the step. Sadan showed me his feet, which ended in smooth, rounded stumps instead of toes. 'I met the Brands too late to save these,' he said. 'But they gave me shoes that let me walk.'

In a high-pitched, singsong voice, Sadan told me wrenching stories of past rejection: the classmates who made fun of him in school; the driver who forcibly threw him off a public bus; the many employers who refused to hire him despite his training and talent; the hospitals that turned him away with a brusque 'We don't treat lepers here.'

'When I got to Vellore, I spent the night on the Brands' veranda, because I had nowhere else to go,' said Sadan. 'That was unheard of for a person with leprosy back then. I can still remember when Dr Brand took my infected, bleeding feet in his hands. I had been to many doctors. A few had examined my hands and feet from a distance, but Drs Paul and Margaret were the first medical workers who dared to touch me. I had nearly forgotten what human touch felt like. Even more impressive, they let me stay in their house that night, and this was when even health workers were terrified of leprosy.'

Sadan then recounted the elaborate sequence of medical procedures – tendon transfers, nerve strippings, toe amputations and cataract removal – performed by the Brands. By transferring tendons to his fingers, they made it possible for him to write again, and now he kept accounts for a programme that gave free leprosy care through fifty-three mobile clinics. He spoke for half an hour. His past life was a catalogue of human suffering. And the stigma continues to this day: just recently he had sat in a car alone and watched his daughter's wedding from a distance, afraid his presence would disturb the guests.

As the Brands and I sipped our last cup of tea in his home, just before leaving to catch a plane to England, Sadan made this astonishing statement: 'Still, I must say that I am now happy that I had this disease.'

'Happy?' I asked, incredulous.

'Yes,' replied Sadan. 'Apart from leprosy, I would have been a normal man with a normal family, chasing wealth and a higher position in society. I would never have known such wonderful people as Dr Paul and Dr Margaret, and I would never have known the God who lives in them.'

* * *

Two days later, our reception in England made for a striking contrast to the royal welcome we

had received in India. There, too, Brand and I
retraced the steps of his past. We visited the
ancestral home where his missionary parents
had spent their furloughs. His mother had
come from wealth, and the house, located in
one of London's better neighbourhoods, was
easily worth a million pounds. Its upper-class
occupant came out to see what we were staring
at, and Brand treated her to a room-by-room
tour, describing how the house used to look
sixty years before.

That afternoon we stood on the hospital
roof where as a medical resident he had fire-
watched during the German bombings. No
one garlanded us with leis and no one gathered around us to sing hymns and give
testimonials. To the guards and staff workers
at the hospital, Brand was a confused old man
interfering with their work. Offices had
moved, wings had been torn down, security
procedures set in place. In the setting of his
early medical career Brand seemed, if anything, an anachronism. We wandered from
receptionist to receptionist at University
College Hospital enquiring after former faculty colleagues. 'Who? Could you spell that
name?' was the typical response. Finally, in a
darkened hallway, we found a row of photos
of some of Brand's teachers – doctors who
were as famous in their day as Christiaan
Barnard or C. Everett Koop are in ours.

I caught myself wondering how Paul Brand's career might have played itself out had he stayed in London. Even working in a remote Indian village among outcast leprosy patients, he had achieved world renown. If he had stayed in a research capacity at a well-equipped laboratory, who knows what honours might have come his way. A Nobel Prize, perhaps?

But what then? His picture would join the others in the darkened hallway, now dusty and beginning to yellow. His name, like theirs, would appear as a footnote in the medical text-books. Fame in the annals of medicine rarely lasts long; microsurgery techniques have already outdated most of the procedures considered breakthroughs in Brand's youth. In contrast, his work as a missionary surgeon in India continues to bear fruit, in the transformed lives of Namo and Sadan and hundreds like them.

Coming so close together, the encounters in India and England became for me a kind of parable contrasting the transience of fame with the permanence of investing in service to others. Whether we live out our days in India or England or Clarkston, Georgia, the true measure of our worth will depend not on a curriculum vitae or the inheritance we leave, but on the spirit we pass on to others. 'Whoever finds his life will lose it, and whoever loses his life for my sake will find it,' said Jesus in his proverb most often repeated in the Gospels. Each career path offers its own rewards. But after sitting with Brand in the homes of Namo and Sadan, and then touring the Hall of Fame at the Royal College of Surgeons, I had no doubt which rewards truly last.

In one of our last conversations, Dr Brand turned reflective. 'Because of where I practised medicine, I never made much money at it. But I tell you that as I look back over a lifetime of surgery, the host of friends who once were patients bring me more joy than wealth could ever bring. I first met them when they were suffering and afraid. As their doctor, I shared their pain. Now that I am old, it is their love and gratitude that illuminates the continuing pathway of my life. It's strange – those of us who involve ourselves in places where there is the most suffering look back in surprise to find that it was there that we discovered the reality of joy.' He then quoted another saying of Jesus: 'Happy are they who bear their share of the world's pain: in the long run they will know more happiness than those who avoid it' (translation by J. B. Phillips).

Dr Paul Wilson Brand, orthopaedic surgeon, who was born in southern India in 1914, died on 8 July 2003 from complications related to a subdural haematoma.

From SOUL SURVIVOR by Philip Yancey
Copyright © 2001 by Someone Cares
Charitable Trust
Used by permission of Doubleday
a division of Random House, Inc.
UK Publisher Hodder & Stoughton

ISBN: 0-340-78601-9

MATT ROPER

Matt Roper is a journalist working in the human rights field. He is the author of the popular *Street Girls*, about rescuing the victims of child prostitution in Brazil with the help of the charity Signpost International. In *Remember Me, Rescue Me*, he returns to the same country to investigate the underworld of the street girls and its links with criminals and mafia leaders.

Governador Valadares: The 1.99 Girls

by Matt Roper

'You simply can't do the trip without coming here,' Abigail had insisted when I rang her to tell her about my plans.

Abigail was the leader of the Children's Council in Governador Valadares. I had known her since my work with street girls in Belo Horizonte. Many of the girls who lived rough on the streets of Belo came from Valadares, making the journey hidden inside freight trains bound for the state capital. Through our work some of the girls returned to their homes. But for every girl we sent home, another one or two arrived back on the streets. There were five children's councillors working full time in Abigail's department and they could not cope with the number of new cases that arrived on their desks every day.

Valadares has a number of attractions that have made it an unlikely tourist centre. For example, the town has some of the most peculiar winds in the world. Hang-gliders and paragliders from all over the world come here, attracted by the huge *cumulo-mugus* – hot air that rises in strange twists and creates unusual turbulence. A number of international competitions are hosted by the town, the most spectacular of which is the hang-gliding World Cup.

Valadares is also famous for its semi-precious stones. Hidden beneath the lacklustre landscape, encrusted in underground caves, are some of the world's richest reserves of gems and minerals. Diggers come from all over the world to chisel out their own specimens. And those whose mineral tastes are more scientific than cosmetic come to scour the ground for meteorites from Mars. In 1958 one of the only ten 'red planet' rocks ever discovered was found in Governador Valadares.

I arrived on the outskirts of the town and for a diversion (and a cool respite from the morning sun) drove up the Ibituruna, a plug of volcanic rock that juts out from the flat river valley. A group of reluctant hang-gliders was preparing to leap from a 1000-foot-high cliff edge. After more than an hour, none of them had summoned up the courage to make the jump. Rather disappointed, I made the steep descent back into the stuffy mid-morning heat and spent the rest of the morning window-shopping in the few busy town-centre streets.

The Valadares shopper has really only two choices of where to spend his or her money: the gemstone shops and the 1.99 shops. In the former you can buy rough and cut stones of every size and type – green tourmalines, red rubies and bright blue topaz, and none of them selling for less than 100 reals. You can also buy mineral sculptures, delicate figurines of genies, goddesses, aliens, bears and other strange creatures fashioned in minerals like jasper and dolomite.

The 1.99 shops are crammed with plastic toys, furry animals, fake mobile phones, cut-price clothes and hundreds of other cheap Paraguyan imports, all for a single, knock-down price. They are the commonest shops in town and, to judge by the crowds of shoppers rummaging in the bargain bins, the most popular.

They were also more within my price range than the gemstone shops, and I spent most of the rest of the morning there. I bought a furry pen with a flashing top and carried my trophy back to my hotel, the São Salvador.

In the afternoon I went to see Abigail. Her desk was piled high with files and folders. She gave me a bleak run-down of the situation in Valadares. In 2000 the Children's Council had attended 184 cases of child prostitution involving children of between ten and fourteen years of age. By the end of 2001 the number had soared to 400 and was still rising. And these were only the cases that had come to the Council's attention – the real figure was cert-ainly much higher.

'What does that name mean?' I pointed to a folder on Abigail's desk that bore the scribbled label '1.99 girls'.

'It's the nickname they give to girls who sell their bodies on the motorways. You've seen those 1.99 shops that sell all those hideous cheap things?'

I hid my flashing pen.

'They call them the "1.99 girls" because they're cheap and worthless. That's what they say – and the girls end up believing it.'

I looked through some of the files and read some of the stories they contained.

Janete – fourteen years old, living with her father, mother and three brothers. Her father organised drinking competitions for his sons and gave prizes to the one who downed the most beer or cachaça rum. When drunk, Janete's brothers often beat her up or tried to rape her. At twelve she had begun to let men grope her for money. Now she sold her body on the motorway, often leaving home for days on end. She had been to the Children's Council three times looking for advice about sexually transmitted diseases she had contracted.

Sabrina – sixteen. Her mother had been a prostitute and had died when Sabrina was seven. Sabrina and her brother had gone to live with an aunt who was constantly shouting abuse at her. She often said, 'Go to the motorway like your vagabond mother!' As soon as she could, Sabrina left her aunt's house and went to live with a group of female friends. Every night they went to the motorway, where they sold sex to truck drivers for just ten reals a time. Sabrina was pregnant and had no idea who the father was.

Sâmia – thirteen. She was found by the Children's Council renting a room in a cheap town-centre hostel. She said she had come to Valadares from a nearby town to make money by selling her body. She claimed her parents did not care about her. Angry that the Children's Council had foiled her moneymaking scheme, she ranted, 'I've got lots of clients in high places – businessmen, even policemen. So don't think you're going to stop me.'

'Do you think I would be able to talk to one of these 1.99 girls?'

Abigail thought for a moment. Then she handed me a file. 'That's Leidiane,' she said. 'She's thirteen.'

Leidiane lived in a huge favela shanty town on the outskirts, called Tourmaline. It was a vast eyesore. Named after the translucent gem-stone by somebody with a warped sense of humour, Tourmaline was a squalid collection of shanty shacks and red-brick buildings strewn haphazardly over a huge mound of red earth. It looked like a giant mudslide, with people crawling over the hillside like ants, and vultures circling overhead. The dirt track to the foot of the hill ran between the motorway and the open-top refuse tip. The mound itself was criss-crossed with electric cables. Close up, the shacks perched precariously on the muddy slopes. Rubbish was piled in heaps along the track; at places the stench of rotting animal carcasses bit at the back of my throat, making me choke.

I located Leidiane's house halfway up an almost vertical side of the hill. As I approached the red-brick house my legs were aching. I clapped my hands in the customary way and Leidiane's mother appeared from behind a rotting wooden door. Leidiane was scrubbing clothes on a concrete washboard. She had a baby face, large brown eyes and a bulging belly. At just thirteen, Leidiane was seven months pregnant.

'She's a hard worker,' said her mother, as Leidiane wrestled with slopping garments, banging them against the rough board. 'But she's got a problem. She has a bad nature. I don't know where she gets it from, I really don't. Leidiane, come and talk.'

She put down the washing and told me her story. The oldest of ten brothers and sisters, she often had to look after them on her own; she had no idea who her father was or where he might be, and her mother struggled to find money to feed the large family. She was an entrepreneur in a small way, acquiring used clothes and selling them to other favela dwellers. But there was not much money to be made that way. 'So I began to go on to the motorway,' said Leidiane. 'You can make money on the motorway.'

She was eleven when she began selling her body. She joined three other girls from Tourmaline: sixteen-year-old Solange, fourteen-year-old Jordânia and eleven-year-old Paulinha. Every night this gang of four went to Ceasa, the town's food stockpile, where trucks unloaded their cargoes of perishable goods. 'I charged five reals, sometimes less. It depended how badly I needed the money.'

She had travelled miles up and down the BR-116 motorway, hitching lifts with drivers. 'They would pick me up, pull up in the middle of nowhere, and afterwards just leave me there in the pitch dark. So I would cross over to the other side of the motorway and wait for another truck to take me back.'

One of those truck drivers was the father of Leidiane's baby, though she could not remember which one it had been, and he was probably hundreds of miles away by now. His ten-minute five-real fling with the young 1.99 girl outside Tourmaline was far from his thoughts now. For him it had been a moment's entertainment, like a go on a slot machine or downing a bottle of cachaça. For one poor, frightened girl, however, that night's misadventure would probably cause distress and pain for generations to come. Would the baby – a fiver's worth of unprotected sex – grow up to be a 1.99 girl like her mother?

If good intentions could achieve success, Leidiane was in with a chance. 'I'm going to be a good mother,' she assured me. 'I'm going to bring up my child well. I'm finished with working the motorway. No more thumbing for lifts on the hard shoulder!' She patted her tummy protectively. 'Not like the others,' she said dismissively. 'They're still down at Ceasa every night.'

But the odds were cruelly stacked against her. A few minutes' conversation made it clear that Leidiane knew nothing about being pregnant and even less about rearing a child.

Her mother told me that she herself had been a 'woman of the night'; Leidiane was the unwanted consequence of a cheap liaison in a trucker's cabin. I watched this protective mother and her industrious, house-proud daughter and once again my heart was crushed to see the old pattern operating. So many children I'd met were following in their mothers' footsteps. What chance did any of them have, when puberty was just another earning opportunity and childhood something that passed fleetly by, like a beautiful landscape seen briefly from the window of an express train?

I decided to find the other members of Leidiane's gang. Solange was easy to locate. She lived in the next road. But she was not home when I called. She'd left early, leaving her new-born baby with her mother. 'She's gone to the Black Hole. I get so worried when she goes there. Two girls were murdered there last week.'

The Black Hole was a boca-de-fumo, a place where drugs were bought and sold. Solange, like her best friend Jordânia, was involved with a dangerous gang of drug dealers. The house where fourteen-year-old Jordânia lived, just around the corner from Solange, boasted a cast-iron door. I banged hard. She erupted from her bedroom, her hair – dyed a patchy blonde – tangled and matted. I said I'd come from Solange's house.

'Don't mention that piranha here,' she snarled. 'The bitch accused me of sleeping with her baby's father. As if I'd stoop that low!' This was just a temporary hiccup in their relationship, Jordânia conceded, but in the meantime if Solange dared to come near the house she'd get her eyes scratched out.

The third member of the gang was also not at home when I called. Eleven-year-old Paulinha lived with her mother in a tiny room at the end of a dark alleyway at the foot of the hill, where rubbish and effluent washed down when the rains came. The place stank. Paulinha's mother greeted me suspiciously. 'She isn't here. She's gone to Inhapim. She won't be back until Thursday.'

'What's she doing in Inhapim?'

The woman looked at me sharply, as if suspecting I was being deliberately stupid. 'Why do you want to know?'

There was only one reason why anyone would go to Inhapim, it turned out. The place was a roadside brothel fifty miles down the motorway. Paulinha worked there regularly for two or three days at a time, while her mother waited back home for her eleven-year-old daughter to return with the next month's grocery money.

I trudged back out of Tourmaline. The stifling cocktail of traffic and industrial fumes seemed almost healthy by comparison with the reek of decay and filth that I was leaving behind.

As the precarious heap of dwellings faded into the distance I was lost in thought. How could a mother make her daughter sell her own body? What did sex mean to these young children, used and brutalised from before the first stirrings of womanhood? What lay ahead for them? Would they ever have relationships in which physical love-making was the joy and deep mystery it was supposed to be – or was sex going to be for the rest of their lives just a handful of loose change? And what of those who kept this evil system in place, from the truckers who treated the young prostitutes purely as objects of passing pleasure, to those who could do something to help the girls but chose not to do so?

Like Gideon facing a mighty army with just a handful of men, I wondered what possible impact any individual could have against the faceless, powerful structures that defeated, with frightening ease, the efforts of government, local jurisdictions and the voluntary sector to bring it all to an end.

* * *

Cecília woke from a drugged sleep to find padded silk surrounding her. There was no light, no sound beyond her hoarse breathing. Slowly she began to grasp the horror of her situation. Her plan had worked – worked too well; she'd feigned death to avoid marrying the man she despised and now her true love, Valentim, was weeping inconsolably by her tomb. Which was where Cecília was right now. As realisation dawned she cried out, her voice weak from the drugs, pushing desperately against the pillows and finding only unyielding wood beneath. Above, Valentim heard her faint cries and began digging frantically in the sticky earth until his fingertips were raw and bleeding.

Then the phone rang.

Brazilian TV soap opera is a genre all its own. Most of the plots seem to be taken straight from Shakespeare plays, and the melodrama is piled high. These novelas thrive on the cliffhanger, the teaser that keeps you coming back for more. Lying on my hotel bed I'd been engrossed in the latest episode of A Padroeira, the six o'clock soap, and though I was fairly sure that Cecília was going to survive, the phone was an unwelcome interruption.

'Do you want to help us catch a pimp?'

Abigail's voice was as calm, as if she was offering me a drive in the mountains. *A Padroeira* seemed, all of a sudden, to be no longer so interesting.

'She's called Fátima,' explained Abigail. 'She arranges young girls for tourists. She lives in a squat in a boca-de-fumo, in a warehouse near the river. Meet us at the corner of Parasol Street and Ângelos.'

The whole team of councillors arrived in a minivan driven by Pablo, the Council's driver. 'Here's the plan,' said Abigail. 'You're a foreign hang-glider. Pablo's a hang-glider too. You're here for the gliding event. You want Fátima to fix you up with some young girls.'

Pablo and I approached the warehouse on foot, along dark and empty streets. A steel panel in the warehouse wall had been forced open. We climbed through the makeshift doorway.

Inside it looked like a scene from hell. A cardboard city had been built from boxes and pieces of wood nailed together, dividing the squatters and their few belongings into their own spaces. There was no light apart from candles dimly flickering and blue circlets of gas flames where people were cooking rice and beans. There was no way of knowing how many families were crammed into the dark shadows. Barefoot children were running everywhere, their screams echoing in the vast hollow interior. I asked some of them if they knew Fátima. They ran off to fetch her. A few nearby faces watched us out of the gloom without much interest.

Fátima was gaunt and scruffy, her clothes dirty and ragged. We shook hands and I explained what we wanted. In the noise nobody could have overheard our conversation, but a hidden microphone in my pocket recorded what was said.

'I can get you two sisters. I'll need some time, though.'

'How old?'

'Thirteen and fourteen. They're very pretty.'

'All right. How much?'

'We can talk money when they arrive. Half goes to me, half to the girls.'

'OK. What time do we collect them?'

'Come back in an hour and a half. I'll go and get them right now.'

It seemed we had a deal. It was eight o'clock. We had until nine thirty to get the police into position and decide what to do next. I asked Fátima one more question. 'Might there be a problem with the police? We don't want any trouble . . .'

'Oh no,' she assured us. 'No problem at all. The police never bother us here.'

Fátima clearly did not suspect a thing. When Pablo and I returned to collect the girls, Abigail and the rest of the Council team were waiting in a police van parked just around the corner. Abigail rehearsed me for my big moment. As soon as Fátima handed the girls over I was to give the signal. The police would then move in and catch her red-handed.

My heart was racing as we climbed once more through the narrow gap in the warehouse wall. I knew that if anybody suspected that we were informants we would be in very serious danger. Inside the place was darker and much quieter. The air was filled not with the stewing of beans but with the strong smell of cannabis. Fátima appeared from behind a curtain. Behind I could see a group of men, sitting in a smoky mist, taking drags on a joint. She seemed different now, less businesslike and more relaxed. Much more relaxed, I realised; she was slurring her words.

'C'mon, let's share a joint before you go,' she said languidly. She nodded towards the smoke-filled room. The men looked at us. There was no way I was going further into that darkness.

'Uh - no, we're in a hurry, I'm afraid. Got to get back. Haven't we, Pablo?'

Pablo nodded furiously. I was already feeling trapped. My heart was beating even faster. As Fátima considered my hasty apology I wondered for a moment if our cover had been blown. Then, to our enormous relief, she shrugged her shoulders and went to get the girls.

They followed her out of the gloom. Both were short and plump, both had matted Afro hair, both wore Lycra shorts and top. They were sisters: Valcelene and Valdirene. We emerged into the street, followed by the girls. I took Fátima to a nearby streetlight to talk about payment.

'Fifty reals for each girl,' she said, her eyes daring me to challenge the exorbitant price. She was relying on my ignorance; as a foreign tourist I might not know that you could get a young girl for a tenth of that without looking very hard. If I wanted to argue I would get the rough edge of her tongue, of that I was sure.

But I didn't want to argue; the money would never be paid anyway. Fátima handed over the girls and I produced my wallet.

It was the sign the police had been waiting for. The van hurtled round the corner, lights flashing and siren blaring. Everybody froze as it screeched to a halt. Four policemen leaped out, shouting and waving their revolvers. We

were all arrested and thrown inside the police
van.

It had been decided that for Pablo's sake our
real identities would not be revealed to Fátima
and the girls – Pablo, as the Council's minibus
driver, was a regular visitor to Fátima's part of
town. It would be very dangerous for him if he
were ever recognised. So we both remained
handcuffed in the van for nearly three hours,
while Fátima was taken into the police station
and formally charged.

We overacted terribly. Pablo was the worst,
wailing and sobbing heartrendingly. I added
my own grief. 'What am I going to do? I'll miss
the competition tomorrow.' I plunged my head
into my hands and groaned dramatically. I had
picked up a few acting ideas of my own from
Cecília and Valentim.

'We're being arrested – and you're thinking
about flying?' exclaimed Pablo.

Next to us, Abigail was trying to pretend she
did not know us. But she was barely stifling her
giggles. The police too joined in the amateur
dramatics: one pretended to hit Pablo in the
face, using the old theatrical trick of slapping
his own hand with his fist. Pablo screamed like
an Oscar winner and the girls winced in horror.

Fátima was certainly not pretending. She
was dragged, weeping and wailing, to a cell in
the police station basement, where she would
stay until her court hearing. The evidence – part

of which was the tape recording I had made –
was overwhelming. According to the Penal
Code, Fátima was due for three to eight years in
prison for the crime of procuring minors for
prostitution.

The two girls were returned to their home. It
was explained to them that they must attend
the Council's Sentinela programme that provides counselling and occupational therapies to
child victims of sexual exploitation and abuse.

Sentinela is a state-sponsored scheme based
in the towns and cities with the highest inci-
dence of child prostitution. It works from
centres that are very well equipped and staffed
by expert counsellors. The programme is an
example of the huge efforts that the Brazilian
government is making to deal with prostitution. The case of Fátima, on the other hand, is
an example of how the efforts of the state are
constantly being thwarted by corrupt local officialdom, by police who turn a blind eye, and by
other people along the line who benefit from
the continued existence of this tragic trade.

A few days later I saw Valcelene, the younger of
the two sisters, again. She wandered into a bak-
ery close to my hotel while I was sipping a shot
of strong coffee. She tried to slip away without
my seeing her. I called her over. 'It was a set-up,'
I explained. 'Pablo and I were plants. It was all
rigged, just to catch Fátima.'

'I knew it! You were all laughing too much.'

'My bad acting, I'm afraid ... Would you like a Coke?'

She told me her story. The girls' father had abandoned them while they were babies. Their mother had been shot dead earlier in the year. Their older brother had run up debts with the drug dealers: they'd come looking for him with guns. His mother had shielded his body with her own, taking the bullet that had been meant for him. 'She was just like that,' said Valcelene. 'She'd do anything for us.'

After their mother's death the sisters lived with their brother, who was still an addict. He paid for his habit by street fighting and burglary. 'There's never enough money for food. If we didn't have what I and my sister earn on the streets, we'd starve.'

She was pleased, she said, that Fátima was now behind bars. Fátima, who was a pimp for hundreds of girls, kept most of the money for herself. If I actually had paid fifty reals for Valcelene, she would only have received a few reals of it.It was a story that was becoming too familiar: Valcelene and her sister had turned to prostitution because they had very few options, and Fátima had exploited that lack. But there was a glimmer of hope. The sisters were now being mentored by professionals at the Sentinela programme. If Valcelene and Vadirene really wanted help, they were now no longer on their own.

* * *

I had reached the end of my week in Governador Valadares. It was time to return my hired car and take the gruelling three-day bus journey to Recife, on Brazil's north-eastern coast, over 1000 miles away.

Before I left, I went back to Ibituruna for the opening of the hang-gliding championships. The sky was cloudless and crystal blue, like a topaz stone. I watched a glider make a running jump over the edge: he floated gracefully into the distance, then climbed in spirals, up towards the dazzling sun.

I thought how many tourists come to Governador Valadares to fly overhead or to burrow underground; yet few know what is really going on at ground level. Thousands of young girls have been tossed into the bargain bin of prostitution and branded with a name that means 'worthless and disposable'. Most of the 1.99 girls ended up believing it.

Yet it was the price tag that was really worthless. To God these lives were worth far more than the richest exhibits in the gemstone shops. Not one of those children, huddled in darkness waiting for the brief trauma that would put a few coins into the family purse, was unseen by him. The biblical image of the sparrow, whose fall is seen and grieved over by the Creator, has never seemed so apt as it did when I visited the homes and workplaces of the children who were being exploited. Truckers brutally using pre-pubescent girls – mothers forcing their children into prostitution – children whose childhood was being destroyed by nightmare experiences of murders, drugs and violence – and perhaps worst of all, the brief account in Luiz Ribeiro's files of the virgin auction in Montes Claros.

I had tried telephoning my tip-off, Carlos, every night from my hotel but had had no luck. I decided that I would not leave Valadares without making one more effort to contact the elusive Carlos. But I met with exactly the same brick wall. Nobody wanted to put me in touch with him, and I was as far as ever from finding out more about Cláudia and her highly placed 300-strong clientele.

My characteristic impetuosity suddenly kicked in. I made a snap decision. I would postpone my trip to Recife for a few days. I would go back to Montes Claros to look for Carlos. The virgin auction was too big a story to abandon. It was a prime example of people in authority, implicated in shocking abuse of children, and protected by corrupt local officialdom. Find the end of that particular string, I reasoned, and it might lead me further into the heart of the darkness whose fringes, I knew, I had barely touched.

From REMEMBER ME, RESCUE ME
by Matt Roper
Copyright © 2003 Matt Roper, published by
Authentic Lifestyle
an imprint of Authentic Media
PO Box 300, Carlisle, Cumbria, CA3 0QS, UK
and PO Box 107, Waynesboro, GA30830, USA
www.paternoster-publishing.com

ISBN: 1-85078-479-5

DAYNA CURRY AND HEATHER MERCEER with STACY MATTINGLY

For 102 days the lives of American aid workers Heather Mercer and Dayna Curry lay in the hands of the Taliban. If they were found guilty of trying to spread Christianity in Afghanistan, they knew there was a possibility they could be put to death. *Prisoners of Hope* is the dramatic story of their ordeal and how their faith supported them in times of darkness.

Bombs, Birds, Cats and Mice

Dayna Curry and Heather Mercer with Stacy Mattingly

Dayna: On the evening Atif and Bismillah left with our notated copies of the charges, I had not been out in the courtyard long when I heard footsteps. The gate opened. Najib and another man were leading a woman wearing only a headscarf into our building. I could not see her face. Another prisoner, I guessed. Some days earlier, guards had put two young Hazara women, one with a ten-month-old baby, into the spare room on our hallway. The women were arrested for interacting with some strange men - men not related to them - in connection with a carpet purchase, we were told. Perhaps this new woman was brought in for not wearing a burqa.

Najib took the woman into the building and I went back to talking with God. Some moments later, Diana called me in to help translate. Inside, Najib and an official who had journeyed from Jalalabad were trying to talk to a very frustrated Westerner. Her name was Yvonne Ridley; she was a British journalist.

Heather already had been translating for some minutes when I came in.

'Will you please ask these men where I am and what they're doing with me?' the woman asked.

Yvonne explained that she had been transported to our prison from Jalalabad under the pretence that she would probably be flown out of the country from Kabul airport. If she did not end up flying out, the men told her, then she would be able to stay with some foreigners in a really nice hotel.

'They have satellite television, access to videos and computers, and all the food they want,' the guards promised.

Well, she had been lied to.

'This is the first time I've lost it,' Yvonne explained to the six of us. Today, 4 October, was day seven of her captivity after being arrested for sneaking into Afghanistan under a burqa without visa or passport. She had come into the country undercover for her newspaper, the *Sunday Express*, to report on how the Afghan people felt about the coming war. She was forty-three years old.

'When can she leave?' I asked the men, acting as translator. 'When will you fly her out?'

Najib and the official did not give a clear answer. 'We will be back to talk with her. We will be back tomorrow.' Tomorrow was Friday, the day of prayer, an unlikely day for progress on her case.

Najib went to retrieve a *toshak* and blanket for our new inmate, and Yvonne came with us to our room. Tears streamed down her face.

'They've finally broken me,' she despaired. We were her first female company since her arrest.

Yvonne told us she heard about our plight on the radio in Jalalabad. She said she also heard Mullah Omar was asking President George W. Bush to reconsider bombing the country in return for our handover. She remarked that the offer was a pipe dream for Mullah Omar.

'I expect America to bomb this week,' Yvonne opined, noting the presence of 3000 journalists in Pakistan positioned to report on an attack. 'It's not a matter of if the US will bomb, but when. You must brace yourselves for it.'

Yvonne proceeded to enumerate the dreadful details of the 11 September attacks on New York and Washington DC. With horror and awe, she described the collapse of the Twin Towers and the sheer desperation of the people who jumped from the upper-storey windows to escape fires and massive explosions. Passengers on the airplanes used their cellphones, she said, to call their loved ones and say their last goodbyes before the planes crashed. She talked about the incredible courage of the passengers who took their aircraft down in a Pennsylvania field to prevent the hijackers from using the plane as a missile. She told us of the young man, Todd

Beamer, who said to the passengers 'Let's roll' before crashing that plane.

The details overwhelmed us. We were gripped with sorrow. We had known the attack was serious, but now we had images – and they were gruesome. For the first time we could vaguely comprehend the emotional nightmare through which our country was living. Our hearts broke for the grieving families. We were also saddened to hear that some Americans were reacting against foreigners who looked Arab or Central Asian. Fear had taken hold.

I was awake in my bed for hours that night; my heart physically hurt. We had spent a lot of time praying for the American families who lost loved ones back when we first found out about the tragedy, but now we felt the impact of the events in a profound way. How could we dare to hope the President would hold off bombing for the eight of us when so many had died? Action needed to be taken against Osama bin Laden. Our lives were in God's hands. If we perished, we perished.

We gave Yvonne a place to sleep on the floor, making sure she was comfortable, and told her she was welcome to have breakfast with us in the morning at seven o'clock.

The next morning Diana made the grocery list, adding a carton of cigarettes for Yvonne. Yvonne warmed up some water and took a bucket bath. She was covered in mosquito bites

and taking medication. Then she asked to bor-
row some of my make-up so she could feel a
little more human.

'Eyelash curlers!' she exclaimed, noticing I
was holding a pair. 'You have eyelash curlers.
How wonderful!'

Officials at the prison in Jalalabad had given
Yvonne a little kit of toiletries and a fancy white
dress covered in gold sequins and beads. We
asked her what she was doing with a wedding
dress. 'I thought it was a bit elaborate for prison
wear,' she quipped.

Najib came to our room that morning with
another man. They asked Yvonne for her last
name and some other information for prison
records. The cook needed to know how much
food to prepare, Najib explained.

Yvonne would not co-operate. 'I refuse to talk,'
she said. I was translating. 'I am not going to eat
anything until I am out of this place.' Yvonne
was on a hunger strike. She had threatened to go
on a no-bathing strike, but we begged her to
refrain – Heather was already protesting our
imprisonment by refusing to wash. One dirty
person in our confines was enough.

I told Najib, 'I'm sorry, Yvonne is not eating,
so you do not need this information from her.'

Najib was steaming – I had never seen him so
upset. 'Well,' he said, 'I will be happy if she dies.'

'Oh, OK.' I waited to translate until he had
walked away.

* * *

Heather: Atif came back on Yvonne's first full day at the prison and told us he was taking our notes to Pakistan to prepare our case. He and Bismillah would return in a week and present our defence to the court.

I begged him not to go. 'Please, we have no contact with anyone here. No progress will be made on our case if you leave, and the war could start. You might not be able to get back into the country.'

Others pleaded, too. Atif assured us he would be back soon. With tensions escalating, however, I was not so confident.

Before Atif left, I went out to the courtyard to write a note for him to carry to my family. Yvonne was in the courtyard, smoking a cigarette. I cried as I wrote. I was upset that Atif was leaving. We could be totally cut off from the rest of the world if he was unable to return.

Yvonne and I talked for a while and she told me crying was OK. I was truly comforted. I never felt like I had permission to cry. Yvonne let me be free enough to cry without trying to fix me. I was grateful.

I asked Yvonne what she would like me to put in my letter so that word of her whereabouts could be communicated to the proper people. I added a brief paragraph about her at the end of the note. When I went back inside the room, Atif was waiting to leave. Najib asked me directly if I had written anything to my family about Yvonne.

'Yes,' I answered, and he confiscated the letter. I had invested all that time writing to my family and he was taking my letter away. None of us was allowed to include any news of Yvonne in our notes, Najib said. He told me to rewrite my letter. I replied that I could not remember what it said, so Najib gave the letter back and let me copy the part to my parents.

* * *

Dayna: On Saturday, the official from Jalalabad returned to the prison to speak with Yvonne about her ordeal. The conversation proved a less-than-harmonious exchange. Yvonne told us she was going to play it tough. We told her she might end up endangering herself. She did what she had to do to try to get released.

Najib asked me to translate, but I told him I would rather not. He understood and asked one of his men to take my place.

'You can judge a civilisation by its prisons,' Yvonne announced to the men, 'and you people are primitive. This is a revolting prison.' The new translator worked out the phraseology for the official.

'We have been at war for twenty-five years,' the official replied. 'The quality of our prisons is not a priority.'

Yvonne was unmoved and continued to decry the conditions. Taliban guards gathered at the wooden gate and peered through the slats to glimpse the shouting foreigner.

Later that afternoon, Afghani and his deputy came by to speak to Yvonne and deliver letters faxed by our parents. Yvonne was no more cordial than before. Afghani, who spoke fluent English, fully understood her. Lest anyone fail to catch the point, Yvonne spat at the men's shoes.

Afghani came inside and told us about the spitting. He was almost laughing from the shock. 'She is a very hostile lady,' he exclaimed. 'She even spat at our shoes!'

We told Yvonne we did not think our conditions were so bad. 'Well,' she answered, 'you have introduced a very hygienic regime. This is probably the first time that toilet has seen disinfectant in many years.' She said she was full of admiration for our routine and the way we had organised ourselves. We had minimised the potential for disease and other health crises, she noted.

Every now and then, Yvonne came into our worship meetings. She told us our singing lit up the place, that our voices made a wonderful, melodic sound – 'a heavenly sound,' she said.

'When you get out of here,' she encouraged us, 'you all should go into a recording studio and cut an album by the "Kabul Six"'. We laughed at the prospect. If we ever were to assemble any songs for a record, we most certainly would not be the ones doing the singing!

* * *

Heather: Late in the afternoon, heavy gunfire erupted while we were out in the courtyard. I went into the women jailers' room and got under the bed. I did not know what was happening. The shooting and firing went on for more than half an hour. We later were told a US spy drone had flown overhead. The shooting came from anti-aircraft guns on the ground.

I knew the episode meant war was near. That evening Afghani and his deputy returned to the courtyard to see how we were faring after the shooting. They came with a satellite phone. Unprompted by any request from us, they told us we could call our parents. Silke was particularly grateful; she had not yet received any letters from her family, since no adequate German translators could be tracked down in Kabul. For the duration of our imprisonment, the Germans experienced difficulty when it came to getting their letters. Kati, Silke, and Ursula had to remain incommunicado for long stretches, and it was very hard on them.

The phone call made up for the difficult day. We were given unlimited time to talk to our families. I had not spoken to my parents since just before they were evacuated from Kabul, and I was so grateful for the chance to hear their voices again. We caught up on family life, and I told my parents about Yvonne. My dad said he felt confident the US would not bomb Kabul while we were imprisoned in the city. My mother, on the other hand, told me to make sure I kept my wits about me because I would need them. Both of my parents reassured me that I was handling the pressure just fine. I felt like they understood me and let me deal with the crisis in my own way. I relinquished the phone greatly encouraged.

Meanwhile, Najib, Afghani, Afghani's deputy and some other Taliban were sitting in the courtyard. When a newscast reported that an American drone had been shot down, the group cheered. The deputy punched the air with his fist. 'Yes,' he exclaimed. The report about the drone was later declared untrue.

Before he left, Afghani stated, 'I am abso-lutely confident there will be no bombing by America for the next month. Now, for three months, I cannot tell you. But for one month, I am certain.'

The following day, 7 October, Najib cleaned out the storage room across the hall for Yvonne. He ended up taking her to a room upstairs that afternoon, however, and we did not see her again. We sent her on her way with a Ken Follett suspense novel to help her pass the time.

That evening I was sitting in the hallway chatting with Maria-jan. One of the two Hazara prisoners had just gone into the bathroom.

Suddenly, an incredibly loud explosion rocked the place, and the girl in the bathroom flung open the door. Her face froze in an expression of terror. 'Was that a rocket?'

We lost electricity. The two Afghan prisoners went into the spare room and began to cry.

Diana knew right away that the US had kicked off its bombing campaign. I was not sure. Considering what my father had said on the phone, I wondered if perhaps the Northern Alliance was attacking.

I went into the jailers' room and got underneath the bed. I hurriedly walled myself in with *toshaks*, pillows and blankets. I had already removed the glass panes from the outside window and from two registration windows that opened on to the entranceway. I knew that the weight of an explosion could shatter glass into thousands of minuscule slivers. I assumed that if an explosion caused any part of our building to collapse, I would be slightly more protected from debris if I was under the bed. At the very least, the covering provided an element of security. I tried to take all precautions – after all, there was now a war going on.

Meanwhile, I prayed aggressively, trying to keep my focus on God's ability to protect us.

* * *

Dayna: I stood at the door to the courtyard gazing at the fireworks show. The Afghan women inside were crying. Silke, Ursula, Kati and I quietly watched the tracer bullets fly through the air. A red ball would traverse the sky and a red streak would follow it. The whole sky would light up red. The bombing did not seem terribly close, but the anti-aircraft guns were loud.

I heard Heather praying in the jailers' room: 'Thank you, Lord, for protecting us. Thank you, Lord, that you are in control.'

Heather: I remained underneath the bed for some time. I was holding myself together, but with great effort. Lying under the bed was almost like being in a coffin. I would say to myself, 'OK, remember when you built forts as a little girl. You are in a fort.' The whole prison was pitch black. We had a few candles burning in the hall.

Suddenly I heard Diana's voice: 'Oh, my gosh, she's gone into labour! Maria-jan has gone into labour! There is bombing, no electricity, and we're in the middle of a blinking prison!'

I evaluated the desperate situation and I thought to myself, I am much better use to everyone if I just stay under this bed. The best thing I can do is not lose it. The others assisted Maria-jan.

Dayna: Maria-jan was lying down in the hallway next to the bathroom. Her lower back was killing her. Diana was rubbing her back, trying to soothe her. We had given Maria-jan money for the doctor in the past for regular exams. She was having much difficulty with her pregnancy and was frequently in pain. This episode, however, was different from the others.

I was translating.

Diana said: ' Ask her if her water has broken.'

I asked her, 'Is your water broken?'

'Yes,' Maria-jan moaned.

'Ask her how much water has come out. Is it a lot or a little?'

'How much water has come out? A lot?' I asked her.

Quite a lot, Maria-jan indicated.

Diana was exasperated. 'No, Lord,' she prayed. 'I can't deliver premature twins. I can't do this. Please don't let this happen!'

Diana said we would have to try to get Maria-jan some help or get her to a hospital. Diana knew premature twins would die if delivered here. Kati went and called for Najib. Minutes later, Najib and Sonan appeared.

When she saw the men, Maria-jan became defensive. She was embarrassed.

'Tell the boss there is no problem.'

I said to Najib: 'She has just broken her water. She is going to have a baby.'

Maria-jan looked at me. 'That is shameful to say.' These men were not her relatives. For her to be exposed like this was taboo in her culture.

'But these are your children,' I said, pleading with her. 'You are in pain. You need to go to the hospital.'

'I am fine,' she said.

Najib and Sonan asked her directly, 'Are you OK?'

'I will be fine,' she answered.

Then Sonan commanded Maria-jan to stand up. 'Get off the floor!'

She could barely move, but Maria-jan gathered her strength and stood for him at attention.

Heather: The others brought Maria-jan into the jailers' room and laid her out on the bed under which I was lying. We all prayed for her that the labour pains would stop and that the children would survive. She seemed to calm down. The storm of pain had passed. Her water must not have broken. Perhaps the sound of the bombs jolted her into false labour, we thought. Eventually, the others left the room, thanking God.

I stretched my hand up from underneath the bed and grasped Maria-jan's hand. We both cried as she recounted the memory of her children's death during a battle between mujahideen factions.

'I was at work that day wondering if my children were safe. When I returned home, I saw that a rocket had hit my house. I found my two sons dismembered in my courtyard. Their innards were everywhere. Their eyes were gone. My boys were dead.'

'Oh, Jesus,' I prayed silently. 'When will it be over? When will the people of this nation be able to live in peace, without fear, without war?'

My body was trembling. I wanted to be strong and encourage Maria-jan that we would get through the bombing.

'Would you like me to sing a song about God taking care of us?' I asked her.

'Yes, please,' she replied.

I sang in English: 'The Lord is my Shepherd. I shall not want. He makes me lie down in pastures of green. He leads me beside the still waters of peace, restoring my soul, restoring in my soul.'

As I sang softly, the peace of God calmed my heart. I wondered if the song was helping Maria-jan cope as well. Within minutes, I could hear her snoring. The singing must have worked. She had fallen asleep.

Somewhere between nine and ten o'clock Afghani's deputy arrived with a couple of his men. We expected that someone from the foreign ministry might show up to give us information and to ask us how we were doing.

The deputy came to the door of the prison that night wearing a fatigue vest. In one breast pocket were extra cartridges for his Kalashnikov. In the other were extra rounds of ammunition. He carried a walkie-talkie in one hand and a phone in the other.

I went to the door. 'Was that America or the Northern Alliance?'

His response was outrageous: 'There is no war. No one is bombing. They are just practising. Do not worry.'

I almost laughed. 'Those were bombs. Who is bombing?' I insisted. 'Please get Afghani on the phone for me.'

The deputy called Afghani and handed me the phone. 'Afghani, this is Heather. What happened?'

The Northern Alliance had attempted to bomb Kabul, he answered, but everything was under control. 'You are safe,' he said.

I was not reassured. He simply was telling me what he thought I wanted to hear. In fact, we would have preferred to hear that America had bombed the city, since we figured the US would be aware of our location.

The next morning, one of our lady jailers, Roheena-jan, told us American planes had dropped the bombs not only in Kabul, but also in Jalalabad, Kandahar and other cities.

* * *

Dayna: Once the bombing started, our women jailers stayed with us only from nine a.m. to four p.m. They wanted to be at home at night. Bombing usually began at seven o'clock in the evening and occurred in rounds. The electricity would go out, and we would light candles in the hallway. Later, we ordered flashlights from the bazaar.

We pushed our evening worship meeting to a later hour to compensate for the loss of electricity. Silke wanted more time to read before the sun went down and we lost power. To light our room, we placed a candle on the window ledge. One night Najib came down and asked us to put the candle out. He was afraid the planes would see the light and bomb the building. We chuckled. With current technology, the planes would be able to spot the building, candle or no candle. Nevertheless, to placate Najib, Silke usually set a book in between the candle and the window.

In the early days of bombing, Kati, Ursula and I decided we would rather sleep in the hallway to get away from the picture window in our room. Silke and Diana stayed in the room. Their bunk bed was positioned in such a way that they believed glass shards would fly past them if the window blew. Heather began sleeping in the jailers' room under the bed.

At some point, sleeping arrangements shifted again, and I was the only one left in the hallway. Camping solo did not last long. One night a clattering sound woke me up. Mice were jumping around on the metal shelves near the entrance to our room. I could not bear the thought of mice crawling on me while I was asleep. The mice were the last straw. I went back to sleeping in the room.

At first I tied a chawdur to the bed to shield myself from flying glass. I slept on the bottom bunk and tied the chawdur on the metal bed frame between the top and bottom bunks. Then Diana suggested using a board from the storage room to make a wall at the head of the bed. We also cracked the window to release pressure so the glass would be less likely to shatter in the event of a close explosion. Finally, Diana ordered thick, clear tape from the bazaar and taped big asterisks over the window to prevent glass from shattering into the room. I stopped using the board at that point.

Since the women jailers were gone at night, we convinced Najib to allow us to lock ourselves in the building. He reluctantly conceded. We explained to him that being locked in from the outside while bombs were dropping would make us very nervous. We might need to get out of the building, we said.

One night, several weeks into the bombing campaign, we were having our worship meeting in the hallway when we heard a rattling sound at the door. We knew someone had locked us in. We stopped singing. Everyone became very nervous. Heather went to check the door. As we suspected, it was locked. Then she went to the jailers' room and started calling into the court- yard, hoping Najib would hear from his office.

'Sir, sir – we need more water! We need more water from the pump!'

Heather went to the bathroom and emptied some of our containers so she could have them ready. We always needed water at night to flush the toilet.

A man came down to the door. Kati and Heather went to talk to him. 'Let us talk to Najib. We do not want this door locked,' they said. Najib came down and a discussion ensued.

Silke looked at me where we were sitting in the hallway. 'Dayna, they need you to go and talk to him. He likes you.' I got up.

Najib was explaining that he was afraid for our safety. He said something about some Kandahari Taliban possibly coming to the prison to harm us.

'Please,' he said. 'This is for your protection. I love you as my sisters. We need to do this.'

I explained that many of us would be very nervous if he locked us in. 'We will not open the door unless you come,' I assured him. He gave in.

'Do not even open it to me,' he said. 'Do not open it to anybody.'

After that incident, Heather and Diana wanted to damage the metal loop for the padlock.

'That would be destroying the place,' Kati and I said. 'It might get us in more trouble.'

They came up with another idea and wrapped rope around the metal loop so there would be no room through which to slide a padlock.

At night in our room, we could hear men pacing the floor above us and talking on their radios about the bombing. Georg told us Najib had built a small trench out in the men's courtyard for protection.

One night a loud banging sound in our room woke us up. I froze. *Kandahari Taliban*, I thought. *They are coming to harm us.*

Moments later, we realised that a cat had gotten into our room and was hurling itself against the glass. The cat looked wild. I hid under the blankets. Brave Kati opened the window and let the cat out.

Heather: Normally bombs would drop for twenty minutes, then stop for a couple of hours, then drop for twenty minutes, then stop, and so on throughout the night. Often we would hear a whistling sound and then an explosion. Sometimes we could hear aircraft overhead, then the whistling and then the explosion. We always heard gunfire.

One night we were having our worship meeting when a bomb struck so close that it blew the doors to the bathroom and spare room wide open. The explosion frazzled us. Dayna jumped into Silke's arms.

Sleeping through the bombing proved nearly impossible. Dayna and some of the others took sleeping pills. I tried the pills once, but they served no benefit. Every night I was so wide-eyed, anticipating the next round of explosions, that I could not fall asleep. All night long I would lie under the bed in the jailers' room and look at my watch. My stomach would tense up. My body would not relax. I passed the time by singing worship songs, praying and thinking of my family. I always knew another round of bombing would come. If I could just make it to five a.m., when most of the raids ceased, I knew I would be able to sleep for a few hours. Once the day strikes started, I barely slept at all.

By the time we got to the second prison I had deteriorated emotionally. I was exhausted and did not know from moment to moment whether I would be able to keep going. I thought I would rather die than continue on in such pain. I tried to hold on, but the more I tried, the more desperate and abysmal my existence became. I faced a crucial decision. Either I could quit wrestling with God and trust him, or I could continue fighting against fear's unyielding grip on my life and in the end surely die from the anxiety and grief.

I feared that if I gave God the power to decide whether I lived or died, then he would take my life from me. I was not certain God wanted me to live as badly as I did. In the end, the exhaustion served me well. I was too tired to keep wrestling. Though I could not see the way ahead, I chose to surrender to God. I gave up. I threw myself into God's hands.

I wrote: 'Lord, all I can do is throw myself in your hands and say have your way. I am utterly desperate and I can do nothing, so I put my life in your hands. By now I've gone numb. It's as though I can't take any more, so I just have to shut down. God, I trust you! Lord, you're my only hope. I resign now and ask for your grace to endure ... Oh God, I want to live, but my life is in your hands. If I live, I live for you. If I die, I die for you. In the end, you are in control and you have the last word.'

My resignation released incredible freedom. The grip of fear began to loosen. I still struggled, but my spirits lifted and hope for my future returned. At times I even believed we might make it out alive. Even so, I ceased putting my hope in the end result of our crisis. My hope rested in the promise I had for eternity. Whether my natural life ended in prison or not, I knew I would live forever in heaven with Jesus. Though the Taliban could imprison my body, they could no longer imprison my spirit. I experienced freedom within, and I could go on.

While at this major spiritual crossroads, I remembered a dream that I had while travelling to Afghanistan for the first time in 1998.

Though we were headed to Kabul during peacetime and my heart was filled with joyful anticipation, in the dream I was deeply afraid. God took me in an elevator to a point above the city of Kabul. I prayed fervently and God told me to look down. The city was being bombed. Then I saw myself walking through the city. God was directing me: turn left, turn right. The route I travelled was confusing and unpredictable. Each time I took a step, the place where I had been standing got hit with a bomb. War broke out all around me; yet, at every point, I was one step out of harm's way. God was showing me exactly where to go.

When I remembered this dream, I recognised it as a foreshadowing of my prison experience. The recollection helped me overcome fear. I believed God was indicating that I would come out alive and unharmed. After some time I told the others about the dream. They were encouraged and jokingly said, 'If anything happens, we will make sure we get behind you!'

We enjoyed some light moments in prison. One night I was reading with a candle in the hallway and writing letters. Everyone else was getting ready for bed. I had some bread beside me on a blanket, along with some cheese for a late-night snack. In the stillness I heard our portable heater slide slightly across the concrete floor.

What was that? I thought. No one else was in the hallway, and I knew the heater could not move on its own. I went to investigate, and when I looked back in the direction of my book, I saw my bread had disappeared.

'Diana, come out here!' I whispered loudly.

Diana came with her flashlight and directed the beam on a mouse carrying a long piece of bread in its mouth. The mouse scampered off and disappeared through a hole in the wall near the bathroom.

Neither of us liked mice and preferred to leave this one alone, but days earlier we had ordered a mousetrap from the bazaar. Diana and I decided to set the trap up. We placed it right underneath the hole near the bathroom wall.

In the meantime, Dayna got up to go to the bathroom. Diana and I laughed and warned her she might run into a mouse. The next thing we heard was a piercing scream.

'It's a mouse! It's a mouse!' Dayna cried.

She ran back into the room and jumped on Kati. Diana and I followed her. We feared Najib would come downstairs to see what all the commotion was about.

'I cannot believe you guys get mad at me,' I exclaimed. 'This is crazy. You are totally freaking out, and it's just a mouse!' We laughed. Within moments we heard the loud snap of the mousetrap.

From PRISONERS OF HOPE by Dayna Curry
and Heather Mercer with Stacy Mattingly
Copyright © 2002 by The Hope Afghanistan
Foundation
Used by permission of Doubleday
a division of Random House, Inc.
UK Publisher Hodder & Stoughton

ISBN: 0-340-86121-5

The Dalits of India
A cry for freedom

The Dalits of India have been the oppressed majority for more than three thousand years due to the Hindu caste system. These people have experienced an awakening and are now demanding equal human rights and dignity. They believe that rejecting the Hindu caste system and getting an English education are the keys to finding freedom. On November 4, 2001, the Dalit community gathered in New Delhi and on that day, Indian Christians stood in solidarity with the Dalits in their quest for freedom.

In response to an invitation, Christian leaders from all parts of India have decided to start 1000 Dalit Education Centres. The centres will be placed in strategic locations as requested by local Dalit leadership. Each Centre will cater to the primary educational needs of 300-500 children

and built on high academic standards based on the Christian world view about God, human dignity, human salvation and social equality. Each DEC will have a team of competent nationals of at least five school teachers and ten Bible teachers and pioneer workers.

OM India is looking for international partners to join the work of reaching out with God's love to the oppressed of India through Dalit Education Centres. There are several ways in which you, your fellowship or your foundation can get involved. Some potential partnership agreements include:

- Sponsoring the construction of a Dalit Education Centre.
- Sponsoring the annual operational expenses of a Dalit Education Centre.
- Sponsoring a class of students.
- Sponsoring literature needs.

To keep in touch, or to be informed about the Dalit Education Centre Project, please write to the following address:

Rosemary Morris
 India Ministries Co-ordinator
  PO Box 660
  Forest Hill
  London
  SE23 3ST

om

Operation Mobilisation India

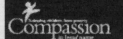

Songs From Around
The World

SONGS FROM AROUND
THE WORLD 2 CD

Various Artists

CD/8203132 Z

A collection of favourite worship songs by a number of international writers
and worship leaders including: Matt Redman, Darlene Zschech, Laurie Klein,
Graham Kendrick, Lenny LeBlanc, Gerrit Gustafson and more!

Authentic
LIFESTYLE

STORIES FROM AROUND THE WORLD 1

Keith Danby (Editor)

ISBN 1-85078-459-0

From Bradford to the Philippines, from Bombay to Romania – each of *Stories From Around the World*'s ten chapters is a testament to God's work amongst the poor, sick and underprivileged throughout the world.

Authentic
LIFESTYLE

OPERATION WORLD

Patrick Johnstone & Jason Mandryk

ISBN 1-85078-357-8

This is the definitive prayer guide to the nations, peoples and cities of the world. Completely updated and revised for the first time in eight years, Operation World provides key background information for every country. Major prayer challenges are gathered direct from hundreds of on-site Christian workers across all denominations. Answers to prayer are carefully logged, complete with all-new maps, cross-references, addresses and indexes. Operation World is the most comprehensive, up-to-date, and wide-ranging compilation of prayer information ever produced.

Authentic
LIFESTYLE

Money raised from

STORIES FROM AROUND THE WORLD 1

went to support the following charities:

Samaritans Purse for Bethany Hospital
Signpost ▯ Oasis
Hope Young Offenders Project
ICC Student Sponsorship ▯ TRIBE Sponsorship
OM UK's 40th Anniversary ▯ NISCU I JAM
Scottish Bible Society ▯ EELAC
CRM Malawi ▯ Carlisle – On The Move
Jubilee Bookshop (Cape Town)
Noel Richards Slovakia Concert
Carlisle – YMCA ▯ Carlisle – Living Well (Raffles)
Carlisle – Trinity School
OM India DEC School ▯ OM India Saji John
Schools Christian Action Team
Peter Maiden Support
OM Turning Point London Centre
Keswick Ministies
Book Project – Native Missionary Project
GV HIV Literature Programme
Tanya Errington ▯ MAD Ministries
OCMS I Bretton Family Project
The Manna House
and Contingency Gifts in the year

JUBILEE CAMPAIGN

Launched in 1987, Jubilee Campaign has for 16 years lobbied on behalf of people suffering as a result of injustice. It is a human rights pressure group, working to protect children's rights and the persecuted church.

Who Says You Can't Change the World?

by Danny Smith

Rescue the Children

Bombay was humid and muggy and I was glad I was only staying twenty-four hours. A 'high-tech' metropolis with real estate that matched New York in price, several blue-chip companies had moved their back-room operations here. I'd spent several months in Bombay as a youth with Operation Mobilisation but didn't think the city had anything special to reveal.

I'd hastily rearranged flights after I'd been urged to visit a local worker. Just an hour after I landed on a sultry evening in February 1996, Reverend K. K. Deveraj led me into the nadir of Bombay's notorious red-light district, a voyage that was only possible because he'd won the trust of people inside the network.

Deveraj had spent over three years helping boys hooked on drugs and consequently learned that their sisters and mothers were enslaved prostitutes. This contact gave him unprecedented access amongst the girls and women who patrolled the back streets and alleys of Kamathipura. Many children from the area wanted to get away, but he had nowhere to take them.

Remarkably, several of the children had developed a strong personal faith and attended church services he held nearby. Some of the prostitutes wandered into the meetings and for that hour business in the red-light district slowed down. For a few minutes, the girls could lose themselves in songs of praise and prayers of hope. Amidst such humiliation and shame, the women responded to this message of deliverance.

By the time we reached Kamathipura, light was fading. I could tell we were close, as girls with heavy make-up in brightly coloured saris lined the street corners in a silent parade.

Fourteenth Lane snaked its way about 100 yards down, a muddy road with narrow houses on the left, mud huts and makeshift shelters on the right. Ramshackle wooden buildings, each a different colour. Hands and elbows leaned on window ledges. Faces peered down. On the street, girls with painted faces, brightly coloured bangles that jingled, jangled. The eyes winked enticingly, but seemed strangely dead.

Deveraj estimated that about 3000 girls lived on Fourteenth Lane and that the Kamathipura area was home to about 20,000 prostitutes, now called 'commercial sex workers.' Bombay, with a population of about 13 million, was said to have over 100,000 prostitutes.

The women in the area trusted him and so I learned some of their stories.

Sharlinka wasn't sure how old she was. She was enticed from Andhra Pradesh with the offer of a job but was sold to a brothel owner. She thought she'd been held captive for about five years, but wasn't sure. 'I had to work hard,' she told us. 'The men were fat, old and smelly. I was forced to do some disgusting things. I wasn't allowed out for three years.'

Another young girl with sad eyes said, 'I'm from Calcutta. I don't have any relatives, only a mother, but I'm not sure where she is now. I drifted around and ended up in Bombay. I was caught one night by several men, they told me they'd find work for me and I'd have a good life but I was sold into slavery.' She had graceful features but a dejected expression. When asked her age she speculated, 'I'm about fourteen or fifteen, maybe even sixteen, but I don't really know.' This girl said she didn't want to go back to the brothel and looked worried. 'I don't have anyone in this world who cares for me. No one knows whether I live or die.'

As she listened intently to Deveraj's words of solace, her eyes widened in silent wonder. It's as though she'd heard about some extraordinary discovery or the plot of an intriguing film. She hung on Deveraj's every word. Tears formed in her eyes. She bit her fingernails.

There were several Nepali girls with pale olive skin, soft features and long angular bodies. Girls were trafficked from Nepal by underworld gangs with police connivance. They were held in a slave market and brothel owners visited the auction to buy the girls. From Bombay, some of the girls – and boys – were dispatched to Goa, now India's most popular tourist resort.

The girls sold to the brothels worked to pay off their debt. Customers paid the brothel and the girls survived on tips. This system of debt bondage kept them in virtual slavery. The girls were held in appalling circumstances, beaten and abused, with little opportunity of ever being liberated from this vicious circle of servitude. In many cases, the girls had no idea when their debt would be paid off – if ever – and were resigned to a life of enslavement. Girls charged between 50 rupees (£1) and 250 rupees (£5) and yes, everything was available with no limits to these sexual encounters.

Bombay's red-light district had a heavy gang influence and there were many stories of shoot-outs and stabbings. Suicides were spoken of factually. Very few got away. Anyone caught trying to escape was beaten severely on return.

One girl, Mina, tried to jump out of a top-floor window but fell and broke her back. She had been caged for seven years and forbidden to leave her room. Usually the girls are kept for two to three years before they're allowed out on their own.

Aids is a time bomb waiting to happen, an explosion predicted by statisticians destined to turn India into one of the major crisis capitals of the world. Predictably, it wasn't hard to find statistics: twenty per cent of Bombay's commercial sex workers were under eighteen and up to fifty per cent of these children were thought to be HIV positive.

To the girls themselves Aids wasn't such a threat. They have problems staying alive. Surviving tonight. Tomorrow was twenty-four hours away.

Night had fallen and the back streets of Bombay were full of girls. A narrow space between the buildings revealed an alley, an active corridor leading deeper into the quicksand. A furtive glance into the warren exposed more verandas, more bright saris, more girls. Somewhere from the midst of the labyrinth, a baby cried, an old man sat crumpled, staring into the distance. Life went on.

Deveraj told me there was a girl he wanted me to meet and we tramped back and forth through the alleys and dark, narrow passageways on a mission to locate her. It was late at night but the streets were crowded and dirty. A woman scavenged through rubbish that was piled up at least fifteen feet high, sprawling everywhere. A child ran across and kicked the garbage playfully. No one stared; no one was surprised.

After twenty minutes, we learned that the girl we were pursuing was at a nearby school where floor space was provided for a few destitute children to sleep. 'She's safe for a few more hours,' Deveraj sighed. 'I don't like her being in this area at night. It's just not safe. Anything can happen.'

The school had locked the gates because of the lateness of the hour, but she was summoned and within minutes an elegant, slender and strikingly beautiful young girl appeared behind the bars of the gates. She talked for a while, while I stayed back in the shadows, observing the scene. In the dim hallway, a coloured light from a nearby neon sign shone on her.

It was hard to define, an inexplicable timeless moment, stirred by an unusual sense of the presence of God. I didn't know her name but felt my heart aflame and planted like a seed within me an affection between a father and a daughter. Here amidst the rubbish, squalor, corruption and oppression, the painted faces, the very presence of a slave kingdom, the overwhelming sense of desolation, she glowed like a precious jewel. I wanted to capture the spirit of this defining moment and the scene around us but it was too dangerous to sneak a photograph. As we retraced our steps and walked back to the car, I heard her story.

Asha's mother was a prostitute who had lived on Fourteenth Lane, just around the corner from us, the street of shame that we'd just walked down. Asha grew up in a cramped squalid room, virtually a cage, where her mother serviced between ten and twenty-five customers a day. Most of the time, Asha and her younger sister and brother were forced to loiter in the street, but many nights she fell asleep, curled up in a corner of the room, waiting for the last customer to leave.

When her mother died, there was almost no time for tears. The brothel owners moved a young Nepali girl into the cage, and Asha and her younger siblings were dumped in the street outside the brothel where her mother had worked. A makeshift canvas hut granted sanctuary from the scorching summer heat and the driving monsoon rain.

The young urchin family ate leftovers given them by friendly prostitutes, scrounged scraps from the rubbish dump, and begged for paisa from passing trade. Their survival was a remarkable record of resilience amidst grinding despair and degradation.

The brothel owners kept a custodial eye on Asha and her sister, as, inevitably, the children of prostitutes always followed their parents into the sex industry. The word on the street was that Asha's mother's boyfriend, a taxi driver, lied and said that he was her father, and was negotiating a deal with one of the brothel owners, expecting about £600 for the sale of this beautiful young girl. That was a small fortune, equivalent to several years' salary, for him. It was money he just couldn't refuse.

The turning point in her life came when she met Deveraj and told him that she wanted to escape. His reply was, 'Have faith. With God everything is possible.' But with each passing day the tension was mounting. She was repulsed by the sexual remarks from local men but there was no escape, nowhere to hide. Every time she spotted the chubby church worker, she chased after him and tugged at his sleeve. 'Uncle! Uncle!' she called out. 'When will you take me away?'

Asha wanted to turn her back on the past. She wanted to wave goodbye to Fourteenth Lane for ever. She told him, 'I want to leave. I feel dirty here. I'll never forget this street but all the memories are bad. I don't like the way the men look at me. Some men want me to join them. They say they'll look after my brother and sister. I sense the danger. Every day it's getting harder for me to live here. I know I can't fight them for ever. It's a question of time. I want to leave here but I have nowhere to go. No one wants me except the brothel owners.'

The next day, Deveraj had arranged for some of the girls, including Asha, to meet me at his office and I was struck at just how young and fragile the children seemed. They were dressed smartly with their hair done and one by one they lined up against the wall and I took a portrait photograph of each of them. Asha, the oldest of the children, was last. She faced the camera. Her eyes were alive with the half glint of a smile. The awkwardness of the meeting, the formality of the soundings and the stilted conversation conveyed little of their circumstances.

It was time to leave Bombay and as Deveraj drove me to the airport I asked what would become of Asha.

'The daughters of prostitutes have all followed their mothers into the sex business,' Deveraj said. 'Very few get away alive.'

'But could she be rescued?' It was the question that I carried with me.

Deveraj felt that the only way to make a difference was to establish a residential home outside the city where orphaned and abandoned children of prostitutes could find sanctuary. It seemed an insignificant gesture given the scale of the problem, but if we couldn't rescue Asha, it was clear she would be condemned to a life sentence of sexual slavery.

On the flight back home, the image of Asha alone in the red-light district haunted me. With it came the realisation that if we were unable to purchase a building, the doors of another house would open for Asha and her life would change for ever.

It was a question of time, a race that I was convinced we must win.

* * *

A Home for Asha

Backstage politics created tension within the office circle, as there seemed an unwillingness to support the project. I took the materials home and, over the weekend, we bundled hundreds of letters that I personally signed, with photographs from my trip, and mailed them out. Although the photograph of Asha wasn't 'dramatic', it seemed to have an anointing as many people were moved and responded generously.

This had become a personal mission and I treasured each response and every pound that came in. As with other projects, one hundred per cent of every donation went directly as designated, and within a few months our prayers were answered – we hit our target. Deveraj located land two hours outside of Bombay and personally designed a grand house that was built in record time. Finally, we had a home for Asha.

Asha collected all her belongings into a cardboard box and waited at the corner, and when the car pulled up to rescue her she climbed in and never looked back at Kamathipura's Fourteenth Lane. Five other girls came with her, including her sister. Her brother also went.

The money came from various sources, mostly individuals with small, sacrificial gifts. One of the larger gifts came from George and Olivia Harrison after it was agreed that a portion of the sales from the Beatles' Anthology project would be donated to charity. With George and Olivia's gift, through the Apple Foundation, we were able to pay the entire running costs for the home for a year.

Sometime earlier, Steve Brown, Billy Connolly's manager, called and asked if we needed money as they had announced a benefit concert during Billy's five-week sell-out residency at Hammersmith's Apollo Theatre in 1997. I sent Steve three projects to choose from. Minutes before Billy walked on stage, Steve told him about our plans to build a home for orphaned and abandoned children of prostitutes and showed him Asha's photograph. Billy walked on stage clutching her photo and for the first few minutes of the show talked movingly about

Asha and explained where the money from that night's performance would be spent. He then delicately placed Asha's photograph on the stool beside him, commenced his act, and within minutes had his audience in stitches. While 3000 people in the theatre were crying with laughter, almost falling out of their chairs, I sat riveted in my seat in the tenth row with tears of joy rolling down my face. I could see Asha's photograph in front of me. She seemed to be looking directly at me. She was smiling.

Billy's concert produced a phenomenal amount of cash. We had the choice of playing it safe and keeping the money for several years' running costs for the home, or we could build another home so that even more children could be rescued.

Within a few months a second equally impressive home was built, again from Deveraj's original design, and over the next few years more than seventy girls were rescued from Bombay's red-light district. Each one told a heartrending story. If it wasn't for this extraordinary work, these girls would be condemned to a life of perpetual enslavement.

When I raised the difficulty of recurring operational costs for both homes with Steve, he came up with the brilliant idea of launching Tickety-Boo Tea, with all the profits used for the project. In October 1999 Billy Connolly invited the media and friends for a day on a tea clipper that sailed down the Thames to launch the innovative idea. Everyone who buys Tickety-Boo Tea contributes toward the running costs for the homes. Even I became a tea drinker.

It hasn't been easy for Asha. She was hospitalised for TB, struggled with her studies, found it hard to fit in with the others in the home, and experienced predictable teenage problems. Although cheerful and bright, she had a melancholic side, and one evening when I was in Bombay she told me, 'I'm sad, but I don't know why.'

Overcoming tremendous obstacles, she enrolled at one of Bombay's top colleges. But the students found out about her background and she had to endure their taunts. She was resilient and strong and faced her accusers head on – a challenge she eventually triumphed over.

In 2002 she married Sanjay, and Deveraj gave me the honour of giving Asha away – one of the most special days of my life. Sanjay worked with Deveraj's team and had known her for several years. The wedding was planned for 25 June but it was also the day that the newspapers predicted would have the heaviest rainfall of the monsoon season. Everyone prayed that the rains would be delayed by twenty-four hours and, with extraordinary timing, the cloudburst came just hours after the reception ended.

Both Asha and Sanjay are now employed by Jubilee Action, working with Deveraj's outreach programme for poor people in Bombay. Deveraj's vision has been inspiring and over time we have developed a unique partnership with his organisation, Bombay Teen Challenge.

* * *

The local municipality in the red-light area were impressed with Deveraj's work and offered us premises to operate a night shelter for the children of prostitutes. The shelter was ideally located in the centre of Bombay's sex industry and would provide prostitutes' children with a safe haven at night, the moment of greatest risk. The children would be fed, get basic medical attention, Christian counselling and encouragement to attend school. The shelter would give us a foothold right inside the sex trade and increase our team's influence in the area. It would enable us to keep a watchful eye on these children as they grew and help to prevent them from entering the sex business.

The property required refurbishment, but before we released funds for the work to be completed I asked Deveraj how we could be sure it would be used for those at greatest risk. The question was answered – like many others – with a telephone call.

'There's a baby for sale in one of the brothels. She's about to be sold,' the man said. 'Come quickly or it'll be too late.'

Deveraj charged out of the office and raced to Kamathipura.

The nine-month-old girl's father worked as a street labourer, the poorest of the poor, in Bombay's bustling vegetable market. Tragedy struck when the child's mother died. In turmoil, unable to cope, and with intense financial pressures, the father took his daughter to Kamathipura, the centre of the sex industry.

The man toured the brothels and, in a moment of madness, offered the baby for sale. The news caused a mini sensation as the brothel owners bargained over the innocent child. The man was offered £150.

The money was a significant amount for the labourer. Just as he was musing over the deal, Deveraj burst into the airless room located at the back of one of the brothels. After some discussion, Deveraj realised that the labourer was determined to sell the baby. Taking him aside, Deveraj warned that there would be consequences and convinced him not to sell the child. The father eventually handed the girl into our care.

Deveraj accepted the child immediately. Any hesitation would have been catastrophic and the child would have been sold.

The rescue completed, the baby was safe. She was named Glory. She was taken directly to our shelter, the first child to be given refuge, evidence of the need and the triumph that faith brings.

I was in Bombay as this remarkable story unfolded. I held Glory in my arms shortly after her deliverance and thanked God for the miraculous timing that enabled Deveraj to rescue this special child. It was wonderful that this millennium baby should be given freedom and a new life at the beginning of a new century.

ISBN: 1-85078-517-1

COMPASSION UK

Compassion exists as an advocate for children: to release them from their spiritual, economic, social and physical poverty; enabling them to become responsible and fulfilled Christian adults.

Compassion began its ministry in Korea in 1952. Now, over 50 years on, it works in 22 of the world's poorest countries, aiding nearly 500,000 children through sponsorship. Compassion links one child with just one sponsor with whom they can develop a personal friendship through letter writing.

Compassion in Uganda

by Ian Hamilton and Kate Smith

In a way I wish I weren't the one telling this story. I will fail every time to show you what it is to live like those on the brink of survival. However, I can tell you of the part we can play in their journey, and the joy it entails. If you could hear first-hand of the daily struggle called normality; if you could see the squalor called home; if you could see the delight and hope amidst the shadows of pain, you too would want to share in their triumph. To be a sponsor of a child in desperate need gives the likes of you and me the chance to do just that: share in a life.

I cannot tell you what it feels like to be a victim of poverty. As much as I can live alongside and talk at length to those who have lived with poverty, I will always have an escape route. Their experience is so alien to the luxury of my own life that I would be foolish and arrogant to suppose I could ever retell their tale. But when immersed in a country like Uganda you do not have to look far to be convinced that we need to do something.

My time spent in a small fishing town in Uganda called Gaba, which lies on the shores of Lake Victoria, was where I met with poverty but also with the hope that is known as 'Compassion.'

* * *

Uganda has a complex and troubled history. While tales of the horrors inflicted on the people by the notorious dictator Idi Amin are no longer current topics of conversation, it is easy to see how the ethnic division, economic degradation, oppression and violence that Amin and a string of other dictators inflicted on the people have brought the country to breaking point. Perhaps this is best illustrated in the journey from Kampala Airport to the city centre. The journey takes you along streets lined with coffin makers and is testimony to the prevalence of death in a society wracked by the pandemic of HIV and Aids. Death is quite literally a trade. At present 710,000 people are living with the disease and over 800,000 children have been orphaned.[1] Recent education and health initiatives have seen the contraction rate of HIV drop quite remarkably, but the problem will not be going away in the near future, and Uganda remains one of the worst affected countries in

---

[1] *The State of the World's Children* (UNICEF, 2003).

the world. In addition to the threat of HIV and Aids, Uganda plays host to over 178,000 refugees from neighbouring countries such as Sudan, The Democratic Republic of Congo and Rwanda.[2]

Despite this, Uganda is a lush and beautiful country. I fear we have been conditioned to see the word 'Africa' as being synonymous with arid deserts and children crying in the dust. But Uganda is teeming with life. The country contains valuable mineral reserves, copper, gold and cobalt, plentiful stocks of fish, as well as magnificent scenery. The misuse of the country by the likes of Amin and Milton Obote saw such reserves neglected, but industry in Uganda is once more becoming a global force under the governance of President Museveni.

I will make my focus Gaba, a fishing town on the shores of Lake Victoria. This small town, rural in every aspect of life, was hit harshly by policies and politics that were imposed from a higher level. The collapse of the nation's economy led to the destruction of the fishing industry here and drove a generation of young men and women to despair. Families disintegrated as men travelled to the city in search of work. Many such men took second wives in the city, perpetuating the spread of what has become

---

[2] http//www.cia.gov/cia/publications/factbook/geos/ug.html.

the world's greatest killer: HIV and Aids. Alcohol and drugs became an escape route for many, and women were forced to subsidise the family income through prostitution. Childhood was snatched from many youngsters when they too were sent out into the workplace. By all accounts it was a place which could be compared to Sodom and Gomorrah.

Within this world of hopelessness, Peter Kasirivu was leading a small church of just fifteen. Peter and his congregation were intent on changing Gaba and slaying the dragon of poverty. When considering the size of the battle Peter and his congregation faced, the match between David and Goliath makes for a good comparison. What chance of change was there in Gaba when Peter and his church were greeted with fierce opposition, which frequently took the form of physical violence? Despite the mountain that faced them, there is no one on earth in a better position to fight poverty and minister to the people of Gaba than Peter Kasirivu.

What makes a guerrilla army so dangerous in jungle warfare is not its high-tech equipment but its knowledge of the landscape and understanding of the conditions in which it fights. In a similar sense, Peter and his church are equipped with an understanding and an experience of the struggles in Gaba that no outsider could ever learn.

And so we have Peter Kasirivu, a man intent on sharing the love of God with his own people. Peter knew that if the words of the gospel were to fall on open hearts then they would have to be seen in practice. An old Greek proverb says that 'you cannot reason with a hungry belly,' therefore, to open their ears, Peter had to feed the people.

The BBC recently ran a programme searching for the greatest Britain of all time. The top ten comprised largely of individuals who devoted their lives completely to one cause, be it sport, music, science. They were people with a passion that gave a purpose to their lives. If we broaden our horizons beyond the shores of our own country, then who would we say are the heroes on a global scale? Ghandi, Martin Luther King, Mother Teresa? These are people who lived their lives as witnesses to their cause.

I think I am justified in placing Jacques Masiko in this category. As the Ugandan Country Director for Compassion, Jacques Masiko stands for all that a charity called Compassion should. The word 'compassion' like the word 'pity' is so often seen as a passive term, inspiring emotion but not action, but compassion should be action. The theologian Matthew Fox considers that 'Compassion is not sentiment but is making justice and doing works of mercy. Compassion is not a moral commandment but a flow and overflow of the fullest human and divine energies.'[3] If you can imagine the kind of person who embodies all aspects of this statement, then you have an image of Jacques Masiko.

Jacques heads over one hundred projects across Uganda. He is very realistic about the plight of Ugandans, but determined that change can and will come. In fact, his plan is to minister to over 50,000 children by 2010; a goal fuelled by his own traumatic experience of poverty.

Jacques is living proof that the cycle of poverty can be broken. At the age of seven he acquired his first full set of clothing and from then on he saved and scavenged to put himself through school and college. The business knowledge and experience he gained had entrepreneurs and corporate directors knocking on his door, but Jacques chose the less glamorous job of working alongside those the country, and the world, had forgotten. The impossible miracle that is Jacques' life drives him on with immense thankfulness and love.

By some coincidence, which I'm sure can only be the intervention of God, the paths of Jacques Masiko and Peter Kasirivu crossed. Jacques had access, through Compassion, to the one thing that was preventing Peter's dreams from

---

[3] www.compassion.org.

getting off the ground – money. During 1990 Jacques and Peter worked to establish a community project run from the church in Gaba that could provide healthcare, education, food, clothing and social care for the needy children of the town. At first just sixty-four children were registered in the project, but as the town slowly began to see God's love in action the project and the church grew beyond belief. The establishment of the project in Gaba is consistent with the establishment of the other 2500 projects that Compassion supports in 21 of the world's poorest countries. The base is always the church, a framework around which the projects can rise. Churches have an accountability that no other organisation can provide and as we seek to build the Kingdom of God it seems appropriate that we should work through his church.

Gaba, as I saw it in 1998, bore little resemblance to the town of hopelessness of twelve years earlier that Peter and Jacques recalled. The church now boasts a congregation of over 1000 on a Sunday morning, a primary school educating 620 students, a high school with 300 entrants and numerous other ministries. Peter takes the greatest delight, though, in recounting the stories of individual lives that have been transformed. He speaks with joy of one man who was an alcoholic town chief leading the fierce opposition to Compassion in the town.

This man is now a church leader reaching out to others with hope, all as a result of a few individuals taking an interest in the lives of the children.

Gaba's transformation is something to celebrate, but the story is by no means over. We need to remember that change here, like anywhere, is not instant and requires continual nurture and development. Long-term change takes years and years. If our desire is to be more than an ephemeral glimpse of joy in the life of a child then we must invest in his or her long-term development.

Let us leave Gaba for a while and head for Uganda's capital city, Kampala, where a group of young adults form part of Compassion's Leadership Development Programme. Compassion's mission is to 'release children from economic, social, physical and spiritual poverty and enable them to become fulfilled Christian adults.' I'm pretty sure that the fifteen young adults I met in Kampala were the men and women that the founders of Compassion hoped would be leading their projects when they wrote this statement fifty years ago.

I won't pretend that every student who leaves Compassion's sponsorship programme has the chance to go to university, but where students have the academic ability and the strength of character they are encouraged to apply for the Leadership Development Programme. University education in Uganda is painfully expensive and way out of reach of the majority of the population, but it remains the place where those with power and influence in a country are educated. As with so much of the work I have seen on my trip, it is not that Uganda lacks talented individuals or the passion to change, but rather the financial investment into human lives.

* * *

I will stray briefly from the lush campus of the university in Kampala to a rubbish tip somewhere on the outskirts of Guatemala City. The air is painfully close, and this is made much worse by the stench of rotting refuse. Birds peck at the scraps of food that lie between the plastic bottles and cans, while rats swam in the stagnant pools emanating from the tip. In the midst of it all you can see small children, some barely old enough to walk, looking for their lunch in the rubbish. It was here a few years ago that Compassion's President, Wes Stafford, took a number of major donors from the US. On arrival at the dump one generous and well-meaning donor refused to leave the safety of the bus. He saw the poverty, he saw the desperate situation of the children, and he was moved and overwhelmed by the atrocity of their situation. So much so that he could not see beyond the pain of their circumstance. He could not see how these children, who were living like the rats, could ever have a chance of a full and joyful life. He saw no point in investing in them.

Later that evening the same donor met a group of Leadership Development students who were studying on a similar programme to those I met in Kampala. During the meal he met a young woman who had just qualified as a doctor. This young lady had spent the first part of her life scavenging with the children on the same tip he had visited earlier in the day. Her life is testimony to the fact that there is always hope.

* * *

Back in Kampala I encountered this same kind of hope, evident in a young woman called Jackie. When she was aged nine, Jackie and her family were made homeless. Her father died after suffering with Aids, and patriarchal laws gave her uncle full control over the family's possessions. He sold the simple shack they called home and everything within it. I feel that my description of their situation as 'bleak' falls rather short.

Yet once more I find myself in admiration of the staff who work on the ground level in Compassion's projects. These project workers

live within the communities we seek to serve
and have knowledge of their community,
which enables them to identify highly vulnerable children like Jackie. Jackie was invited to
join the project; her mother found employment
as a cook in the student centre and was assisted
in finding a new home for her family. A chain of
these small 'acts of love' has transformed
Jackie's life and that of her family. In the future,
through Jackie, who knows how many more
children will be given chances they could only
dream of!

Compassion's focus has always been on children, but it is amazing how reaching out to this
generation gives access to a whole community.
In 2002 UNICEF held the first international con-
ference where children from across the globe
gathered to debate what was important to them.
Historically, children have been marginalised;
seen but never heard. No one understood or
implored this need to focus on children more
than Jesus. When Jesus gathered with those who
were revered and deemed to be important, he
focuses not on them, but on the children (Mark
10:13). This is an example of Christ giving us
some practical advice. Children are the future,
and if we are seeking to build a future Kingdom
of God, then the children need to be a part of
this. When we are told to 'train a child in the
way he should go, and when he is old he will

not turn from it' (Prov. 22:6), we should really take heed.

Most people who come to know the Lord do so between the ages of four and fourteen. Children of this age are more open to learning, they are more willing to share what they have with their families, and Compassion's partnership with local Christians ensures that the spiritual development of a child is of paramount importance. When children know their true worth in Jesus Christ then their lives blossom.

Jackie is now studying mass communications at university and her dream is to fight the injustice and oppression within her country. She told me she wants 'to become a very great woman' and to make a differece in her family and community, and I have no doubt that she will do exactly as she says. Jackie has seen God transform her life beyond all belief. When she speaks of the sponsor who wrote to her and encouraged her when she was a shy nine-year-old coming to terms with the death of her father, she speaks of her 'saviour.' For Jackie, her sponsor is doing exactly what Jesus taught: she is planting a mustard seed.

During my brief time in Uganda I encountered numerous children, most of whom will never have the opportunities Jackie does. Some were playing happily with their friends in the street, some were selling peanuts by the roadside, some were shining shoes for money, and others looked at me with pleading eyes and open hands. This is the face of poverty that greets you every day, but this is remarkably 'pleasant' in comparison with the more repulsive poverty that lurks behind the closed doors of sweat-shops. I did not see the children who are chained to workbenches all day long, cleaning mechanical parts; I did not see the children who risk their lives running in and out of large machines; and I did not see the red-light districts where children sell themselves. Nevertheless, where you find poverty, you find exploitation of this kind. Children who have to work to survive are not qualified for the 'nice' jobs and must take whatever they can to make a few cents. Despite the fact that they live adult lives in all but their age, there are no laws to protect and safeguard them. When I think of these children I think of an old proverb that claims 'you do not have to be old to be wise.' What these eyes had witnessed I dare not contemplate.

It is not practical or realistic to suggest that each of these children should be given the chance of a university education. We need for a moment to remove ourselves from a Western mentality and remember that employment opportunities in Uganda are very different from those in our own country. For example, in

Kenya, around 400,000 young people hit the formal education market every year, but with only 50,000 jobs available, competition and unemployment are both high.[4] If we are to be realistic about development, then we need to look at the alternatives. We need to be convinced that no child should have to live his or her life in the bondage of child slavery, and we need to offer him or her practical alternatives.

Back in Gaba, the fishing trade provides the majority of employment. Students who attend the Compassion project are taught about the agricultural practice of fishing and business management, so that they have skills for a trade and secure employment when they leave. While fishing is appropriate for Gaba, it would not be so of a project in, say, Lima, Peru. Here students learn about hydroponics. Lima saw its first spattering of rain in thirty years last year, and the only place where you will see any splash of green is in the gardens of five-star hotels. As a result, children rarely get the balanced diet they require. The practices they learn in the project can be shared with their families and community on a personal and commercial level.

From what I saw, there is incredible work going on across Uganda, but I was unsure

[4] George Mullenix (Compassion's senior research specialist), *Compassion at Work* (Summer 2000).

exactly what part I had to play in the 'global village' we call the world until I met Martin. My family and I had been supporting Martin for a few years prior to my visit to Uganda. I had written to him and ungrudgingly sent my £18 every month, in ignorance of the extent to which this influenced his life.

* * *

When I first began sponsoring Martin, he had a mother, father and six brothers and sisters, but by the time I met him he had been orphaned. Aids had killed both his parents, and Martin's older brother had been prematurely given the responsibility of family breadwinner. Martin's brother clearly displayed a wise head on very young shoulders. Their story is tragic but by no means unique. With 800,000 Aids orphans in Uganda, there are child-headed families in every town and virtually every street. But the fact that this is not unusual does not make one case any less distressing than the next.

I must admit that as a sponsor in the UK I often wondered what on earth I had in common with a small boy in completely different circumstances in another part of the world. Perhaps this is evidence of the preoccupation we have with 'difference'. In a lecture Bill Clinton gave in December 2001 he observed that 'Most of us believe our differences are

important and make our lives more interesting
… but what will be more important in the 21st
century – our differences or our common
humanity?'[5]

I wanted to take Martin a gift when I met
with him face to face, so I brought with me
what I thought any discerning nine-year-old
boy would love: a football and football kit. And,
just like nine-year-old boy the world over,
Martin was thrilled with the gift and keen to
show his new ball and Watford strip to his
friends. And I'm pretty sure this is the reception
I would have received anywhere in the world –
perhaps not every boy would have been quite
so thrilled with a Watford strip, but I think you
understand the point I am making.

And there are yet more traits we have in
common. Despite the frequency with which
death occurs in Uganda, the pain of losing a
loved one is no easier. Just speaking with
Martin was evidence of the love he has for his
family, the loneliness and loss he felt when
his parents died and the hope he has for the
future. All of these are emotions I too can
understand. The external circumstances that
shape Martin's life may be very different from
those that shape mine, but at heart we are very

---

[5] Dimbleby   Lecture   2001,   available   at
http//www.bbc.co.uk/arts/news_
comment/dimbleby/index.shtml.

similar. I wonder why I should be quite so surprised at this when I know we are all made in the image of God.

In light of this I realised just what an impact I had on Martin's life. When I entered his small house the first thing Martin did was to scurry off to find a battered shoebox. In this box he kept his most precious possessions, and amongst them were the letters I had written and the photographs I had sent him. As I became aware of the vital part I played in Martin's life I felt a sense of unreserved humility and gratitude. Not only was my £18 a month supporting him on a physical level; my words of prayerful encouragement were spurring him on as a young man. I think this taught me the true nature of the servant heart. To embark on sponsorship is an immense responsibility, but at the same time it is an immense privilege. When we give we do receive. Every moment Martin spends in the Rubaya Child Development Centre moves him towards a brighter future. He is also getting the chance to be a nine-year-old boy, and indulge in the freedom of childhood.

* * *

My meetings with poverty shattered the 'compassion fatigue' that we often fall prey to. We get lost in the statistics and fail to see the humanity behind the haze of numbers. The

Ugandan Bishop Festo Kivengee watched this beautiful country suffer in the grip of Aids, war, terrorism and injustice, and yet amidst the pain saw Jesus as 'the one who gives new hope.' He also expressed that he 'found it more difficult to minister to those suffering from prosperity rather than poverty' because 'with prosperity comes the deadening façade that numbs the sensitivity.'[6]

I think we are all a little guilty of this. We have governments and global institutions that are responsible for looking after our basic needs as well as managing international issues. Such organisations are vital, but our reliance on them can result in our conviction that anything we do not directly control is someone else's job. We can abdicate responsibility to the point at which we render ourselves useless in changing anything. And if as Christians we are called to be 'salt and light' in the world, then we should be right up there with the change makers.

It is impossible to travel to a country like Uganda and not be shocked and even repulsed by the luxury we have here. It is all too easy to become angry and resentful at what we have, and this emotion can be dangerous. To be eaten up in guilt means to stagnate in frustration. And I have to be honest with you, I enjoy having a car, a nice house, a stereo, and I would not

---

[6] *Christianity Today*, 8 August 1986.

voluntarily exchange my life for Martin's. What I do know though is that the £18 I invest in Martin's life each month and the letters I write to him provide him with a future and a hope that would otherwise have evaded him. Children will continue to be exploited, families will be ripped apart by Aids, and I don't imagine that within my lifetime poverty will be anywhere near extinction. What I do know is that there are rays of hope being brought by the likes of Jacques, Peter and Jackie, and their army that is fighting poverty. We can support them on both a financial and a spiritual level and form that bridge of hope. If the size of the task ever overwhelms us, then I ask that we think not of the statistics but of the individuals like Martin and of the common humanity and vision for the future we all share. We can all participate in what Mother Teresa called 'small acts of love.'

RICHARD WALLIS/ SIGNPOST INTERNATIONAL

Signpost International is a Christian Charity working with children and families at risk around the world. It tries to share the gospel through word and action through child sponsorship, house building, job creation schemes, building and equipping schools and working with street children, and through church-based missions, evangelism and short and long-term mission opportunities.

Back to Africa: Thirty Years On

by Richard Wallis

Led to Zambia, 1973

I might never have gone to Africa had I caught my usual train that summer morning in 1972. I was working as a young department manager at the huge Owen Owen store in Liverpool (I might as well admit at this point, somewhat embarrassed, that I was in charge of ladies' gloves, handbags and hosiery). I didn't know what had possessed me to catch the bus and the ferry from my bedsit in New Brighton to Liverpool Pier Head to work instead of taking my usual train to Liverpool Central. The balding executive sitting in front of me on the bus had left his copy of the *Daily Telegraph*. Now I could check what was on TV that evening! But as I settled on to a deck seat on the ferry, I noticed the paper was folded to the appointments page, and there it was – 'Retail Managers required in Zambia'. Though not yet a Christian, I thanked God. I felt sure this was the opportunity I was looking for to experiment with some ideas I had developed during my time at Liverpool University studying politics, specialising in the culture of poverty. Within a month, I was attending an interview in London. I had told no one.

The day after my interview God spoke to me! One of my hosiery consultants, Debbie, was ill and her mother phoned to let me know. She then added, 'The Lord has a message for you.'

I was completely bemused and asked, 'Lord who?'

Her mother laughed. 'God! And he told me a great opportunity will come your way later this week and he says you must take it.'

I took it. A contract, a successful first driving test, a work permit, my first passport and X-ray plates (to prove I did not suffer from TB), and I was on a plane for the first time – destination Chingola, on the Copperbelt.

Rarely could a person have left to spend five years in Africa so ill equipped. I had only travelled to France and Germany, and my retail experience was limited to stockings and mittens! However, I was full of idealism and passion. Having just seen David Lean's film *Lawrence of Arabia* I was somehow going to become 'Wallis of Africa' and change the world. Big dreams cost nothing.

So began my mini social experiment in the ZCBC store in Chingola, managing a staff team of sixty Zambians. Never had they seen a '*musungu*' (white man) mopping the floors after work, nor had the company van been used to run staff back to the townships in the evenings. Never had a store manager offered to conduct free evening classes or refereed inter-departmental football matches.

One evening, after I had been in Zambia for about four months, one of my staff challenged me. 'Richard, you are a good man. You want to change the world. But you will never change the world. Only changed hearts will change the world and only Jesus can change hearts.' Five days later, I turned my vehicle over several times on a dirt road and plunged into a deep culvert. Squeezing out of the smashed rear window of the crushed car, one of my shaken but unhurt passengers whispered, 'Richard, at least I knew where I would have been going if the car had gone up in flames.' Unknown to me, members of a local church had chosen that very week to meet together at six o'clock each morning to pray for me. Talk about being chased by God! Within a week, I was an 'African' Christian.

No messages received

Those five years as a young Christian in Zambia were a euphoric time, but sometimes God's voice isn't so loud and clear. During those years of childlike adventures abroad, I had married Susan, who I had first met on the infamous Liverpudlian handbag counter. I thought I would have to 'grow up' on returning to England in 1978 with our two children, Christopher and Anna. And coming back home was a huge culture shock. Our third child, Sarah, soon followed and I struggled as I faced the reality of both family and work responsibilities – the inevitable mortgage, the pressures of managing Scripture Union's chain of bookshops, leaving home before six a.m. to commute to London, trying to be an effective father. More and more, I felt like a tombstone when sitting on the pews of my local church. Increasingly exhausted, the passion was gradually being squeezed out of me. Both the bookshop chain and my family grew and flourished, but it somehow felt like I was marking time.

God uses ministers

Eventually, after ten years, and by now scared that life would continue like this, the tombstone went to see his vicar. I told him that I felt that I was past my sell-by date as a retail executive and he asked what I wanted to do with the rest of my life. I had no clear idea, but what mattered most to me was not what I did, but rather having a passion for something. He shared something that proved a wise insight. We expect too much from God over a one-year period, but too little over seven years. But could God rekindle this fire? Did God still have a plan for a life that at forty-two seemed derailed? I would be forty-nine in seven years – I was convinced it was all too late.

Then a new assistant minister, Kerry Dixon, arrived at our church. He told Susan that one day I would be a Bible teacher. That sounded ludicrous to me. All he had heard was me reading the lesson! He had no idea how desperately I tried to avoid any public speaking. Six months later, Kerry led a team, which included Susan, to the shanty towns of the Philippines. While I was grappling with increasingly grim sales figures, a result of the recession of the early nineties, they were encountering Third World poverty and were seeing God at work in ways they had not experienced before. Out of this trip Signpost International was born.

Kerry had a clear vision for Signpost – sharing the good news of Jesus through both word and action with the poorest of the poor. Over a drink with Kerry on a riverbank, I found myself volunteering to assist him with some administrative tasks. The first package I received contained photographs of 900 Filipino children. I was overwhelmed, and soon became responsible for Signpost's first social action project – our child sponsorship programme. Kerry and I were two volunteers with demanding jobs: Signpost International had an annual income of about £10,000 and we helped people in just one city in one country – Iloilo City in the Philippines. But we gave ourselves grand titles. Kerry was International Director and I was Director of Child Support – titles cost nothing!

God uses shanty girls

The Director of Child Support needed to visit the Philippines, and it was there that I met one of our sponsored children, Cheryl Lynn de Juan. An eight-year-old girl with a father earning less than a dollar a day was about to transform the life of a forty-six-year-old man earning almost a hundred times more. She lived in squalid and crowded conditions in a tumbledown shack built on stilts above the sewage of a large coastal shanty town. I was outraged. The night before returning home, I was sharing a room with two others in Manila. By two in the morning I could contain it no longer and shouted, 'It has happened, it has happened, it has happened!'

Stirring from their sleep, the other two asked, 'What has happened?'

I retorted, 'I have the passion!'

Now I had a purpose. The visit to my vicar had eventually resulted in an answer: God had used that grim shanty town to burn his passion for the poor into my heart. And I knew that when I returned to the UK, I would have to spearhead a housing project to relocate some of these families.

God uses chief executives

So where did I go from there? Was the path to full-time work open? Deep inside I was struggling with the real implications of the trip. It would be wonderful to write that I was obedient to God and resigned from my senior management position with Wesley Owen (who had acquired Scripture Union Bookshops in 1993) and become Signpost International's first employee. Two things prevented me from doing so. Firstly, I was worried about my family's financial position, and secondly, I was indecisive when it came to making big decisions. Then Keith Danby, Chief Executive of Send the Light (Wesley Owen are part of STL), invited me out to dinner. I shared with him my inner turmoil and over the next few months he made it possible for me to leave my nest of security. Unlike me, he believed I could fly. By the end of 1997, I was leaving Wesley Owen, and a partnership was born between STL/Wesley Owen and Signpost International that has subsequently contributed so much to the growth of this mission society. The end of 1997 was seven years since I had met with my vicar. God's hand often appears more visible with hindsight.

'This is mission control calling'

Signpost's ministry in other countries started to grow. Matt Roper founded Meninadança in Brazil (the story told in the best-selling *Street Girls*, published by Paternoster in 2001); projects were initiated in Uganda and Rwanda, including a new secondary school in Kigali; and a partnership was formed with Mission Possible, which works with street children in Moscow. Christian resource centres were established in Uganda and Rwanda. In the Philippines, we started a new micro loan project, initiated more housing projects and a Bible college was established.

I sat at my desk as dusk fell on 31 December 1999 and realised that my title of Director of Child Support was no longer a joke title. Somehow, we had become a medium-size mission society with offices in England and Scotland. Signpost's greatest concern was that we were being perceived as a social action charity, while Kerry's original vision had been the proclamation of the word combined with social action. But as far as I was concerned, others could sort out the mission bit – social action was my baby!

My greatest concern that evening was very different. Susan's health was deteriorating. In July 1999 she had resigned as a nurse. Here was one of the most active women I have ever met, with a big heart for mission, going through what appeared to be the most traumatic menopause of all time. It was suggested that an extended period working as a nurse with a medical mission on the Amazon would re-fire her. She left for the Amazon Basin in July 2000 and I joined her in November for her final few weeks there. As I landed on an airstrip in the middle of the rainforest, I knew this would be a significant reunion, but I was not prepared for a reunion with a wife who had become like a dependent child with severe learning difficulties.

Looking back, it is amazing I did not panic. What was wrong with Susan? Why was she constantly hallucinating? Should I return home the following day with her? Why had I not been warned? Instead of panicking, this most undomesticated of men learned to cook, started to clean and even became proud of his whites! This husband who had been cared for all his married life now became the carer. In the midst of this complete role reversal in the rainforest, I encountered God, who wanted another role reversal. To my utter astonishment, he was calling me to mission. This time it was Kerry who encouraged me to leave the secure nest I had built around myself since leaving Wesley Owen. Gradually, I handed over more and more of the social action projects I had managed. One feels surprisingly vulnerable without a full in-tray! This vulnerability increased when I was told that Susan was suffering from the degenerative Pick's disease – a form of premature dementia, which had started five years earlier when she was just fifty. And I felt overwhelmingly vulnerable when I found myself sitting in on meetings with academics and theologians discussing matters such as the theology of mission.

Mission control: all systems go!

It was at one of these meetings in a grand library in London on a frosty January morning in 2002 that I met François Nitunga. There are some people you feel privileged to meet and God knows when we are in need of an inspiring encounter. This Burundian refugee did not strike me as an impressive man as I struggled to understand what the delegates were talking about. However, I am glad to say my first impression was wrong. After the meeting, he invited me to lead a mission in a Burundian refugee camp in Tanzania, close to the Burundian border.

Once again, God seemed to be propelling me forward 'despite' – despite my totally disorganised prayer life, despite my inadequacies, despite Susan's illness. Maybe grace has a whole deal to do with 'despite'. Rarely could a person have left on mission for Africa with such little experience. I had never been to Bible school and had no mission track record. I was no longer an idealist but an idealist without illusions. I was no longer inspired by a film but by an encounter with God to bring a message of hope to the oppressed. A few weeks before departure I handed over the last of the social action projects under my remit to Signpost's new Head of Overseas Operations. God had released me for new adventures with him.

I had travelled overseas a good deal with Signpost in my role as Director of Child Support and had survived some tight spots. I had been apprehended by the police in Belo Horizonte, who had thought I was kidnapping a street child, and just twenty-four hours later almost drowned on the Copacabana. On Mindanao in the Philippines I had been flattened to the ground by a church leader in order to avoid some passing Muslim terrorists and in Rwanda had crossed a bridge charged with sticks of volatile dynamite. Stupidly, once I had caused tension on an African border. So I was surprised to find myself so anxious before this particular trip. My mission partner, Pastor Stuart Merton, and I were to link up with François in Nairobi, the capital of Kenya. The week before I departed, there was a missile attack on an Israeli charter flight on the Kenya coast. Two days before, the British High Commission in Nairobi closed due to a terrorist threat. Suddenly I wished I had not booked a direct flight from Heathrow to save time – a British Airways jumbo jet now looked very big and very British.

As we prepared to land on a warm and sunny African morning I wondered about the local security arrangements; in particular, would the Kenyan Army be patrolling under the flight path? But I was staggered to see that as soon as we touched down we were surrounded by heavily armed jeeps racing either side of our aircraft and that there were armed soldiers every fifty metres on each side of the runway. As we slowed to a halt, the pilot announced that we would be taken to a special secure part of the airport. Clearly we were a target. Then the pilot added, 'We have a special guest with us today, as one of our passengers is President Daniel arap Moi!' And so I was welcomed back to Africa with a red carpet, a guard of honour, a military band and dancing ladies!

Nairobi is not Africa – at least not the Africa I love. Thankfully, we were soon in a six-seater aircraft flying to Mwansa on the southern shores of Lake Victoria where we transferred to an older six-seater to take us to Ngara on the Tanzania-Burundi border. The second pilot was one of those colourful characters who add so much to an African adventure. He was appalled by the amount of luggage we were travelling with and, having carefully weighed both his customers and their luggage, prepared for take-off. He ended his take-off checklist with 'and if all else fails, bail out in Lake Victoria'. Later he made me promise that François would not return with the entire Burundian tea harvest in sacks. I got the message. Next time I will forget the toothbrush.

The scenery was stunning – it was rainy season and the lush green hills rose to almost 6000 feet, separated by deep valleys. Our base was a settlement on top of one of these hills, called Murgwanza, as visitors are not allowed to sleep at the refugee camp. The site was given to the Anglicans when they arrived in 1932, as this highest hill was considered 'cursed.' Cursed it might have been, but it has magnificent views across a valley to the hills of Burundi and Rwanda. Today, the hill boasts a cathedral, mission hospital and primary school. Living conditions were basic in this remote spot and lying in bed, exhausted, each night I wondered if those 1932 pioneers had carried my bed with them on their backs all the way from Dar es Salaam. Before dawn each morning I would hear the rustle of our Tanzanian hosts stoking up the fire, so that hot water was ready in a bucket for the early morning shower. It was truly loving hospitality from such an impoverished people.

The refugee camp was about twenty-five miles from Murgwanza. The Dean of the Cathedral decided to be our taxi driver. He certainly had the knowledge! He was a delightful Christian full of the joy of the Lord in spite of one big problem – his Datsun pickup was terminally sick. I know little about vehicles, but I know when one is dying. We always travelled with our personal mechanic perched in the back; he was called on to perform operations on various parts of the body every few miles. This was all very amusing until one day we were told we would need to travel in convoy with a police escort as there were bandits in the area. Within a few minutes the convoy with armed escort had disappeared over the horizon as we spluttered along trying to negotiate a small hill. Suddenly every boulder along the roadside looked like a potential bandit road-block. Adventures with God are an exhilarating mixture of fear and expectation.

I have a vivid imagination, and for weeks had been trying to visualise a camp with 200,000 refugees. I had been invited to visit two refugee camps earlier in 2002 when on a trip to Goma in the Congo, where thousands had been displaced by a lava flow swamping the city centre. Each of these was a newly established, tented camp with 3000 refugees. But 200,000 is a figure of 'biblical proportions'. I envisaged a camp with a constant swirl of humanity, like rush hour on the London Underground, all bathed in a sort of mystical dust! This excited me as I reflected on the crusades that had been planned. But my first impression of Lukole could not have been more different: mud-brick houses in neat rows, dirt roads which were wide tree-lined avenues, an air of permanence, a measured pace of life. It was a complete contrast from the congested chaos of the shanty towns I had visited in the Philippines or in the African cities of Kampala, Lusaka and Nairobi.

Extraordinarily, my first impression was that of a suburb in the middle of the African bush. And gradually it dawned on me that it had not just an air of permanence but was a place of permanence. The first Burundian refugees arrived after the 1972 genocide with further large influxes from Burundi in 1993 and from Rwanda during the 1994 genocide. Many of the young adults in the camp must have been born there. Like their parents, they largely depend on food handouts from the UNHCR. Worse, they are not permitted to travel more than four kilometres from the camp, and even this small distance was technically illegal; they are 'prisoners' in this bush suburb. Five per cent of all Burundians are 'prisoners' here. Despite fear of violence at night in the camp, each person I spoke to had a much deeper fear of returning to his or her homeland.

François Nitunga is one of the new generation of young Christian leaders who keep pressing on towards a goal despite seemingly insurmountable obstacles. I had also noted this quality in Nathan Amooti, Director of Education for the Kigali diocese, who I had met in Rwanda a few years earlier. We had sent him a few thousands pounds to start construction of the first diocesan secondary school. As soon as I landed, he proudly took me to the site near the airport. I inspected a low wall emerging from the foundations of a small classroom block. To my astonishment, Nathan announced, 'We will start recruiting staff next week and will open in September.' I was travelling with a headmaster from Cambridge and he almost choked. Funds for the building were almost exhausted and it was touch and go if this small building would have a roof by September. There were no funds for salaries, textbooks or even school desks. Despite our concerns, Nathan pressed on, and the school opened in September, educating many who would have left school after primary education. Since those early days, God has provided funds beyond my vivid imagination, and today the school is an impressive complex educating 300 Rwandans. Like Nathan, François has a dream, and continues when most of us would give up. His dream is to prepare a people in exile to return as 'society changers' to their homeland. And what are the obstacles?

A people afraid of returning home, the increasing influence of Islam in the area, the potential decimation of a generation through the Aids pandemic and a critical shortage of funds. Just one of these would have grounded me.

François had asked Stuart Merton and me to train leaders on subjects related to overcoming some of these obstacles – the uniqueness of Jesus, the need for forgiveness and reconciliation, hope, evangelism, discipleship and a call for excellence in Christian leadership. In the afternoons, there were open-air crusades.

I asked François if I could interview some of the refuges during the break after the morning seminars each day. Keith Danby had asked me to write this chapter a few weeks before I left England and I was already musing about it, as STL/Wesley Owen have generously funded most of my ministry costs over the past five years. I thought I could write a piece on the stories of Burundian refugees. These need to be told, but by someone who has greater investigative skills than I possess. The few interviews I conducted produced stories that were painfully similar. The story of one young man I spoke to echoed the experiences of many. 'The militia came to our school one night in 1993 and started to wreck the place and then killed many of my school friends. I managed to squeeze out of the back window of the dormitory and ran

away into the bush. God protected me as I travelled to Tanzania. I heard later that my parents
and younger brothers had been killed in our
home a few weeks after I reached the refugee
camp. The authorities may send me back to
Burundi, and I am very frightened by that
prospect, as I fear I will be killed by the militia if
I return.'

I was asked to preach in a packed church on
Sunday morning. I felt a little emotional when I
first awoke to the sounds of the 'hot water makers,' remembering that my daughter, Sarah,
would be in a refugee camp in Thailand that
same Sunday; she is a missionary there.

The pastor asked, 'If anyone is here for the
first time, please stand up.' I decided not to
stand up (can someone please tell me what is
the socially acceptable thing to do when one is
so obviously a first-timer?) Among the few who
stood up was a seventy-year-old woman. As
she spoke, there was a sudden hush in the
church, followed by cries of joy. She was the
wife of the elderly church treasurer who had
fled from Burundi in 1993. She had crossed
the Tanzania-Burundi border with their niece
the previous night. They had been out of touch
for nine years and there had been the possibility that they would never meet again. This was
a wonderful reunion. It was a poignant
reminder to me before I preached of the suffering that there is in the camp. It also made me

realise how important it was to say that although I may not fully understand these people's suffering, Christ (himself a child refugee as a result of genocide and later betrayed by a close friend before suffering on the cross) most certainly does.

There had been no repatriation of the Burundian refugees but the repatriation of the Rwandans from the camp was almost complete. On our final day, a convoy of about 20 lorries came to collect about 3500 refugees. As I watched the convoy depart, I noticed something on the last lorry. It looked like a skip at our local refuge collection centre – rickety chairs, soiled plastic buckets, bags stuffed with rags, old pots and so on. Then the reality struck me – it represented the worldly wealth of these 3500 refugees as they returned to face an uncertain future.

God still had a few more surprises in store. Our light aircraft landed at Nairobi's domestic airport during a massive tropical thunderstorm. On the way to the international airport our taxi broke down in a flash flood in the middle of an extremely busy highway. Was I really going to die in a huge puddle on a highway in some foreign land? Suddenly a lorry trying to overtake us by going on to the central reservation jack-knifed around us. God protected us from all the speeding traffic by giving us shelter in the armpit of the lorry and trailer.

England, 2003

For some time I have been tempted to preach a sermon entitled 'Burn your sofas'. We are so comfortable and yet often so arrogant. And we have made armchair criticism almost a fine art. Excellence has almost become a God. We are reluctant to move forward because of fear of failure. And genuine encouragement that fosters risk-taking is so rare.

On the wall of my office I have the following quotation from Theodore 'Teddy' Roosevelt, President of the United States in the early part of last century. I know little of the man except that he hunted bears and that this somehow was the origin of teddy bears. But his words remind me of the inspirational Filipino and African Christian leaders I have worked alongside over the past ten years:

> It is not the critic who counts: not the person who points out how the man stumbled or where the doer of deeds could have done better. The credit belongs to the man who is actually in the arena: whose face is marred by dust and sweat and blood; who strives valiantly; who errs and comes short again and again, because there is no effort without error or shortcoming; who does actually try to do the deed; who knows the great enthusiasms, the great devotions and spends himself in a worthy cause; who at worst, if he fails, at least fails while daring greatly.

Far better it is to dare mighty things, to win glorious triumphs even though chequered by failure, than to rank with those poor spirits who neither enjoy nor suffer much because they live in the grey twilight that knows neither victory nor defeat.

May you know the joy of taking risks for Jesus and having adventures with him. By removing eternal risk, God calls his people to continual daily risk.

* * *

This chapter is dedicated to June, Lyn and Rena, who so lovingly care for Susan at our family home and who encourage me to continue to respond to 'mission control calling'.

* * *

Richard Wallis, Head of Missions at Signpost International, would be pleased to visit your church and be 'passionate about Jesus'. Or you may wish to respond to 'mission control calling' and join him on a mission trip. You can contact him by telephone on (+44) (0)1480 469848, by e-mail at wallis@wesley-owen.com or by post at Signpost International, 12 Links Way, St Ives, Cambridgeshire PE27 6DW. For further information on Signpost International, go to www.signpost-international.org.

Part of the proceeds of this book will be used to fund further missions in East and Central Africa.

SALTMINE TRUST/DAVE POPE

Saltmine brings a holistic approach to making a difference worldwide with compassion and integrity through partnerships, projects, personnel development and creative initiatives.

Established in 1980, it is committed to evangelism, mission and the integrity of the family. Using drama and other modes of communication, their workers present the gospel in churches, schools, prisons, youth clubs and universities.

Internationally, Saltmine works in Eastern Europe where it is involved in teaching programmes, support for building projects in churches and children's homes and organising humanitarian aid. Saltmine International also raises money for relief and development projects all around the world.

James's Story

by David Pope

Time Squares, New York, on a very rainy, blustery evening . . . people scurrying hither and thither, most of them making for eateries or hamburger joints and indeed the subway station just to escape the atrocious weather and the incessant battering from wind and rain.

I blinked as the cold water hit my face, but noticed the half-illuminated sign of the facility where the Saltmine Theatre Company were performing a dramatisation of *The Cross and the Switchblade* – the famous story of David Wilkerson's ministry in his lonely crusade to the most dangerous streets in the world.

Gang warfare, drug pushers, pimps and prostitutes – it was in the early 1960s that Wilkerson stepped into this culture, driven only by the compulsion to share God's love and the promise of the Holy Spirit's power. The need and the message have not changed, despite the passage of time, although the problems of the underworld are not now confined to the streets of New York City. They can be found in any urban sprawl across the world.

As I arrived at the venue, the production was underway. Energised by the uniqueness of performing where the original story was enacted, the cast through their enthusiasm and total commitment re-lived the lurid scenes of the New York ghetto. Wilkerson's bravery and unswerving commitment to the cause of Christ loomed large in the production, but it was never more evident than in the dramatic scene when he is confronted by gang leader Nicky Cruz in non-compliant mode! Cruz lunges at the pastor, who moves swiftly out of reach of the switchblade that slices through the air.

> You could kill me Nicky. You could cut me in a thousand pieces and lay them out on the street. But every piece would cry out Jesus loves you. And you'll never be able to run from that.

The atmosphere in the theatre crackled with the power of these words. Of course, time has proved their impact, and Nicky Cruz, having experienced Christ in a deep and transforming way, now travels as an evangelist and preacher of good news. And Wilkerson is still ministering just off Times Square, reaching out to those in need.

But the real impact of this visit was to become evident on my return to the United Kingdom. There is always a tendency to glamorise the more high-profile conversions to faith in Christ. Cruz's story has been the subject of plays, books and a full-length motion picture, and although genuine and real, one is often left wondering if such transformations occur without Hollywood and dramatic manuscripts being involved. My assurance was soon to come!

* * *

James grew up in the West Midlands in England, in the town of Dudley – best known for its zoo, being comedian Lenny Henry's home territory and, more recently, for an earthquake that registered 5.2 on the Richter scale. Nurtured in a Christian home, James attended the local schools and the Anglican church, but soon his peer group introduced him to all the pain and pressure of growing up in a 'laddish' culture, where bullying and fightbacks are all part of the scene.

James tells his own story:

I really struggled with some of the names that my friends began to call me - primarily because I went to church. I felt victimised, and I remember on one occasion being followed home from school. One of the lads landed a karate kick in my stomach and then beat me up. On another occasion, I remember hiding up a tree, but then they started to throw bricks, and things went from bad

to worse. All of this made me switch off . . . I lost
interest in school, which made life very difficult
for me as my father particularly had high expectations of my being able to reach a good educational standard. Things also began to get really
tough at home, particularly as I truanted, and my
teachers would call my parents and find out what
was happening. I did have some friends . . . I
loved football and snooker, and I dreamt of being
a professional football player. I even had a trial
with West Bromwich Albion.

In his early teens James became very disillu-
sioned with the church. It didn't scratch where
he itched, and because his relationship with his
father was under strain, the concept of God
being a father figure made the issue of faith
unrealistic to an emerging teenager. James
chose to opt out of church and Christian commitment.

But the bullying at school continued, and on
one occasion James retaliated and floored the
guy who was bullying him. It was very messy,
but suddenly this incident became the foundation of a new reputation. James had become the
'hero of the hour' for taking the law into his
own hands.

A holiday overseas found James in a difficult situation where a comparative stranger
took advantage of him. Unable to tell his parents, James felt isolated and trapped, and the

abuser blackmailed him into keeping his mouth shut.

> When I returned from that holiday, my attitude changed dramatically. I began to do to others what other kids had done to me. I was always up for a fight, and I guess that it was my turn to become a real bully. I would play up at school. I developed an interest in pornography and became sexually aware and active with girls . . . but things took a turn for the worst during my last years at school. I travelled to Wolverhampton Wanderers away fixtures, but got in with the wrong crowd and began to drink heavily. I became a football hooligan – always up for a fight on the terraces or in the back streets away from the ground.
>
> I left school in the early nineties and then became involved in the 'rave' scene. I travelled all around the country . . . to rave clubs such as Dreamscape and Fantasia . . . dancing the night away, fuelled up on speed and amphetamines. My drug habit began to grow – but it was all false, a pretence, a fantasy. But I remember saying I will be a raver 'til the day I die.

Without divine intervention, that statement would almost have been prophetic! James was trying to hold down a job working with a furniture company, but because of his itinerant and haphazard lifestyle, he soon began to drift in and out of work. He needed £150 per week to feed his habit and to pay for fuel and transport to get to the dance clubs. Locally, drugs were in plentiful supply: on one occasion, the landlord of a particular pub was locked in his own cellar while customers, many high on drugs, helped themselves to the various vintages on offer. Such was life!

> The drug experiences would take me into a spiritual realm . . . a demonic realm, a realm of something that the human mind would never normally accomplish. A fix would last for about eight hours. But I soon began to snort in increasing quantities – and not just at weekends. I would need substances to get me to work . . . I wouldn't sleep. At work, I would use the toilets to snort just to keep myself going.

But James did not lose contact with his family, and when his mum and dad split up he began to adjust to new people coming close to him. He went to live with his Nan, but would admit to feeling deeply disturbed by the marriage break-up that reinforced his feelings of vulnerability and insecurity.

The drug habit then worsened. James began to inject speed, as introduced by the mother of his first child. The drug habit was also beginning to cost, but having met a dealer who was twice his

age, suddenly James found a new hero: someone he thought he could look up to, even
though he now realises the error of his ways.
Thankfully, he always used clean equipment,
but his new 'mentor' would inject him, and he
would get a real rush. He continued to sleep
around, but it all started to get difficult. The
amphetamines were wreaking havoc with his
ability to hold down a job, and he was getting
into debt, which increased his dependency
upon his friends who were also drug dependent.

I had loads of girlfriends – but I never had a lasting loving relationship. I was too insecure and I
simply used people for my own ends. The
mother of my first child was very involved in the
drug scene, and I soon began to use LSD, which
gave me the buzz to steal from shops. I was hallucinating so strongly that shoplifting was all part
of life's challenge.

My personality began to change . . . I became
psychotic, and if I couldn't get my own way I
became very angry and violent. I developed a
reputation of being aggressive and threatening,
and at the age of twenty-one I was not nice to
know!

James's life was on a downward spiral. His
friends were bound together by drug abuse,
and the cocktail of alcohol and speed falsely

insulated James from reality and responsibility. His girlfriend became pregnant; he graduated to heroin and on one occasion overdosed, which gave him the fright of his life.

> The heroin was easy to get, but this was my first experience of a heavier substance, and I over-dosed and slipped out of consciousness and had to be resuscitated. I was very sick and I remember my 'friends' began to panic. They thought I had gone. I didn't realise just how serious all of this was until someone said to me the following day 'you died last night.'

James realises that in all of this he was really searching for something that would make sense of his life. He recognised the stupidity of what he was doing but felt helpless to chart a new course. Two years passed. He was still doing speed but would visit the doctors for sleeping tablets. He even took up boxing and visited the gym in the local town of Cradley Heath to try to channel his anger, and every Saturday he would go to the gym to spar, but the drug habit was relentless and James was firmly in its grip.

> I know at this time that I was desperately unsta-ble. I knew there was something not right deep down inside. It was so crazy . . . but in the midst of all my mental guys, some guys came to my flat and began to smoke heroin. I was very nervous

because of my previous overdose experience, but I took the risk and 'chased the dragon', burning the foil, and as the substance ran I inhaled and suddenly I felt relieved. My problems evaporated, my emotions were numbed and this was a new experience for me without the negative downside. I felt secure; I slept. It brought me into a new era. This time I didn't overdose, and I repeated the practice at least once a week. I used my benefits to get the drugs and the council paid my bills for the flat. Some days I wouldn't even get out of bed.

James continued to live with his pregnant girl-friend in a dingy darkened flat, surrounded by foil – the trappings from his snorting habit and the grim reminder of a life out of control. Within a month of the baby being born, speed and heroin fuelled the highs and lows. He abused his girlfriend, who then left him and took away the child. Jobs came and went. There were one or two brushes with the law, and the police visited his flat and found evidence of his drug habit, for which he was arrested. He was also charged with physical abuse. The latter charge was dropped but he was fined for possession.

And yet, in the midst of all the chaos, James met another friend – Shelley, a sixteen-year-old local girl who was to move in with him. He introduced her to the heroin habit. They both 'escaped' by injecting. Shelley had also experienced abuse, so there was a meeting of minds, and the relationship grew. James was fortunate in one sense (or maybe it was a clear indication that even in all the mess God had his hand on him for a future purpose): although he suffered a bout of hepatitis, he never contracted the HIV virus through his injecting habits, although he would be the first to say that, at the time, Aids was far removed from his thinking.

After a while, James and his new girlfriend were introduced to methadone under medical supervision. Threats from his former girlfriend's family, court orders, visting dealers' houses with a baby son and doing a round of drug dens were now all part of his life. It was really beginning to get tough.

But, in all of the despair, a light was to shine in the person of Richard Carter, the guy who was responsible for prescribing the methadone and who subsequently became the manager of a drug rehabilitation project in Dudley called 'The Warehouse'. Richard, a committed Christian, had been trained by Jackie Pullinger and had himself been a heroin addict in Hong Kong for eighteen years.

James was initially very suspicious of Richard and particularly his spiritual emphasis. Richard's mention of Jesus revived all of the misconceptions that James had taken to heart about the church and brought back negative memories of his upbringing. God, after all, was someone who was committed to judgement, not forgiveness, so this was essentially a substantial barrier in James's mind, but, when the chips are down, you are prepared to try anything, and James, recognising his depressed state, began to wonder whether the Jesus solution was a possibility. He had heard of other drug-dependent people who had been helped by spiritual therapy and so he decided to go back to his mum to see whether she could substantiate that this was a viable road to travel.

Ultimately, it was James's depression that pushed him in the right direction. He met up with his mum at her workplace in Stourbridge and told her that his life was useless, that he was tired of living from 'hand to mouth' and that what he really wanted was to end it all. James was at the end, and suicide seemed to be the only possibility for release.

James's mum was distressed at seeing her son in such a state, but she knew that there was little she could do to help. She decided to give him some money - not enough to feed his habit, but sufficient to help him get some food and other necessities, and James, thankful for her kindness, decided to walk back to Kingswinford, the town where he was currently living.

But that slow walk proved to be a Damascus-road experience. Tired and deeply depressed, James literally cried out to God – 'God, if you are real, come into my life . . . you're my only hope.'

When I get to heaven, I'm going to see if I can convene a meeting for all those who have prayed desperation prayers, and I also intend to bring together all who have been taken by surprise when God has responded to dire need. I am sure it will be an interesting event to say the least! I would certainly be intrigued if Paul showed up to share his testimony and I would take great delight in putting him alongside James and watching them comparing notes! Miraculously – and I use the word carefully – God heard James's prayer. James would recognise that this was a complete step of faith, although he didn't fully realise the potential of what he was doing. It wasn't until later, when he picked up a book written by Colin Urquart – *My Dear Child* – that he began to understand fully what he had done, and, on the basis of his prayer and newfound faith, Colin's writing really began to minister to him. It was James's mum who had given him the book in the first instance to follow through on this 'new spiritual experience'. 'It was really very funny,' says James now, with a glint in his eye:

There we were in my Mum's garage – me, Shelley, Shelley's brother Michael and Adam, her other brother, and my Mum was sitting in the middle of the garage floor reading this book to us. In the midst of all of this, I decided to follow through on Richard's advice, and apply to an organisation that I heard about called 'Teen Challenge'. I heard of David Wilkerson and of his work amongst people affected by drug abuse, so within a week of walking down that long and winding road to Kingswinford, contemplating suicide, I was filling in forms to see whether 'Teen Challenge' could help me.

At the same time, I agreed to go into a secure unit run by Dudley Borough to come off heroin and methadone. It is a place called Bushy Fields and was adjacent to the local hospital. However, I was only there for six days. I signed myself out, but in this time Richard had invited Shelley and myself to visit his church to meet his pastor.

Simon and Keely Bateson, pastors of the church, welcomed James and Shelley into the fellowship and made them feel very welcome. There was something different here. People seemed to be caring. The coldness of religion that James had experienced in his childhood did not seem to have any place whatsoever, even though there was obviously a strong Christian 'feel' to all that was said and done. At the same time, James was also successful in his interview with Teen Challenge, although there was no immediate vacancy to accommodate

him. Simon and Keely went the extra mile and
welcomed Shelley into their home with their
family, taking her away from the pain and dangers of living on the streets. James again
recognised that something was happening and
sensed that God was doing something in his
life, even though he couldn't explain what it
was all about. James had also found that even
in his dire need he could pray for people, and
was amazed that God honoured him. He
became more spiritually sensitive and apprecia-
tive that, after all he had been through, there
was a God who seemed to be extending his love
towards him. During this time, members of the
church kept close to James and visited him in
the secure unit. One night, as they were praying
together, sitting outside the secure unit, God
gave a clear sign that his hand was on James
through a vision in the sky as the sun disappeared below the horizon. The sceptics might
say, 'Hmmmm!' People of faith say, 'Thank you,
Lord!'

Again, James began to realise that some deep
work was going on in his life. Simon invited
James to join his extended family and he and
his wife were the hands and feet of Jesus in this
very important period. James now recognises
that Simon took an enormous risk in taking
both of them into his home, and he now
remembers all the prayer ministry, sometimes
long into the night, that was very much part of

his rehabilitation. Within one month of being in a secure, safe Christian environment, James saw that in the middle of all his struggles God proved his love and faithfulness to them both.

Wednesday 11 August 1999 was a memorable day for the world. It was the day of the eclipse of the sun. But this was also the day James left for Wales to join the Teen Challenge programme. Journeying along with Richard, Simon and Shelley, James was taking an enormous step as he travelled to the Teen Challenge Centre near Swansea. It was on the M4 motorway, as the eclipse of the sun took place, that James sensed that God was now reminding him that he was entering a new phase in his life. It couldn't have been more clear or, indeed, more dramatic. A supernatural phenomenon to underscore a natural work of intervention in a guy who had the potential to make it or break it.

Life at Teen Challenge was not easy . . . strong discipline, supervision, eleven months of programmes with six months of re-entry as part of the plan to help James re-adjust to the challenge of life without substance abuse. No phone calls for the first month in order to help break contact with the past. Phase One included one visit per month of a pastoral nature. You had to keep good time-keeping, dress tidily, keep your room clean. If you messed up you got a 'white ticket', and if you got too many white tickets you found yourself on more washing-up duties or banned from the tuck shop. James admits that, with all that he had been involved with, this was a very tough programme, but he appreciated the principle behind the discipline and began to respond to the expectations of those in authority. He particularly enjoyed the worship and the teaching.

> We had classes every morning from ten a.m. until twelve fifteen p.m. and then each evening from seven thirty p.m. until nine thirty p.m. I did fourteen studies on temptation, and this helped me to understand the impact of the world, but more specifically the power of Christ in my life. I'd get up at seven fifteen every morning, and after thirty minutes of normal routine duties, I would be into the lounge for my private devotions. I now see how this has served me well because in all that I do now my quiet time first thing in the morning is very important to me. I found the first phase of the programme really difficult because I wasn't allowed contact with Shelley, but after a while I was allowed to make some phone calls. I remember those conversations . . . getting excited about God and knowing that the Lord sets people free.

Although Shelley was still in the West Midlands, the tone of her voice was so different, and God was doing great things in her through the local church and particularly through the care afforded to her from Simon and his wife. Shelley ultimately applied to Teen Challenge and was accepted into Hope House, the facility for girls that was also in close proximity to where James was staying. Shelley struggled at first. On a supervised visit to a swimming pool, she deliberately forgot to pack her swimming costume, which meant she couldn't participate, so she was reprimanded, which caused her to give colourful, verbal abuse to those in authority, and that put her back on the programme! Such was life at Hope House. James calls it 'the Shelley attitude.' Anger, or a display of temper, is dealt with, but in a way that encourages maturity and growth. James also remembers Shelley's discovery of faith:

> Shelley became a Christian in the church before we went into Teen Challenge. We were not married at that time, although we knew each other intimately, but we knew that things needed to change. Teen Challenge helped us both grow in God through understanding his word.

Time rolled by. Both James and Shelley did well, but began to realise that their dependence on each other was making it difficult to depend on God. James also had his moments. On one occasion he became angry with a staff member and was put back six weeks in his programme. He also lost his cool with a fellow student, which had disciplinary repercussions. Ultimately, James survived his training, but he certainly didn't find it easy. On his final phase he went back home for a visit and messed up big time: a few smokes and drinks! He told Shelley what had happened and when the news reached the ears of John Macy, who was the Centre Director, he suggested that James make an immediate return back to Wales to be sure of receiving further help. James complied, but he also lost a month on the programme.

Eventually James and Shelley went back to the West Midlands and moved in with Shelley's mum. James was hurting. Sin had tried to claim back some territory and the devil was playing his role of being the great accuser. Doubt and darkness began to cloud James's vision and he even tried heroin once again. Condemnation, guilt, bitterness and despondency took over and it was a wise word of advice that suggested he returned quickly to Teen Challenge.

James was admitted to Keighley – a new Teen Challenge Centre in Yorkshire – and Shelley returned to Wales. James struggled for quite a while, and physically and spiritually he was in a desperate state. The three and half months of being back in the familiarity of the West Midlands, away from the support structures of

Teen Challenge, had taken its toll, but it was the sports programme in Keighley that brought matters to a head. James had to engage in physical activity, and, having declined swimming as exercise, decided to plump for badminton. As a shuttlecock loomed over his head he went to strike it and fell awkwardly, snapping his ankle. The pain was excruciating and the expletives came fast and furious, as did the white ticket! Medical examination confirmed the worst. The ankle was broken and James, hospitalised for a week, had his ankle pinned. He was admitted to a ward at this time, where the hospital authorities continued with his detox programme, and James found himself whiling away his time by reading his Bible. He began to realise that God had put him in a place where he had to listen, and he now looks back on that experience as being critically important to his spiritual growth. Eventually, James returned to Keighley with plaster cast and crutches, but was determined to follow through on what he had discovered from God as he lay immobilised in that hospital bed. Again, it was time to make some important decisions, but it was going to be different this time. Three staff members at Keighley shared their pain and their backgrounds with James, and he recognised that he needed to be open to deep healing for some of the negative experiences of his childhood. James prayed with his counsellor, and, recognising the root of his bitterness, God ministered his love, peace and overwhelming forgiveness in a new and vital way.

'That was a turning point for me,' says James:

> I began to read more avidly and God confirmed his work of grace during my time in Keighley. I then moved to London. Shelley was in Wales, but while we were apart I was moving on in my faith in leaps and bounds and the Centre Manager recognised I needed some extra outlet for my faith. Within three months, I was helping to run the Centre, rather than attending classes. For the first time for as long as I could remember, I was actually holding down a job with responsibility, depending on God for his help and encouragement.

James began to enjoy his newly found independence. Questions flew as to whether his relationship with Shelley was helpful and so he wrote to her suggesting that maybe it was time to end their commitment. Shelley was heartbroken, and James struggled emotionally, but he knew it was very important to recognise where his strength originated. Shelley ultimately accepted James's wish and travelled to Swaziland to help on a Christian programme with disadvantaged children, and it was during this time that she also came to realise that dependence on God – and not on James – had to be a priority.

It was almost like the Abraham and Isaac experience, where God was testing for obedience. In that Old Testament story, it was the ram in the thicket that eventually paid the ultimate price, but not before lessons and prime loyalties had been affirmed. And so it was with James and Shelley. Seven months later they were re-united after God had proved himself to them in different ways. James was now working driving the Teen Challenge bus, showing responsibility and doing a great job. When Shelley and James came back together, under the direction of pastoral care and wise leadership, they received all the support and encouragement that they needed and that indeed was vital and necessary. The happiest day in their lives was 6 April 2001 when they married at Wollaston Free Church. What a time of celebration! Leaders from Teen Challenge and the local church entered into a wonderful spirit of thanksgiving. James had been encouraged to find an ordinary job for twelve months prior to this happy occasion – working in a steel factory, making pallets, in order to test his calling and his ability to resist temptation and weakness. He came through with flying colours, and so when the chance came for him to take on the role of Supporting Housing Officer at Teen Challenge in London he rose to the opportunity.

Shelley is now taking on a post with a girls' centre in East London, under the direction of Teen Challenge, although her prime role is fulfilled as a mother and housewife. James still drives the Teen Challenge bus and spends time ministering to people who are drug dependent – taking hope and love on to the streets.

James and Shelley live by faith, looking to the Lord via Teen Challenge to meet their needs.

London is a crazy place to live and very expensive – but God is proving his faithfulness in so many ways. We know we are doing what he wants us to do. God has taken away my desire for substances. I am truly dependent on him, and satisfied and fulfilled in a way that I never thought possible.

* * *

I found my time with James to be one of the most enriching and exciting experiences that I have had for some time. Honest, frank, non-triumphalist, real and meaningful – perhaps more poignant, because the pain was worked out on my own doorsteps, my home town, along the streets I have walked many times. What a reminder of the challenge of mission within striking distance of our homes and the need to be good news first and foremost where God has placed us. James's story is a solemn reminder that India, Africa or South America should not always be our first port of call!

KATHY HICKS/
OPERATION MOBILISATION

Operation Mobilisation works in more than 80 countries, motivating and equipping people to share God's love with people all over the world. OM seeks to help plant and strengthen churches, especially in areas of the world where Christ is least known.

Scaling the Wall: Overcoming Obstacles to Missions Involvement

by Kathy Hicks

The Ultimate Sacrifice: The Testimonies of Bonnie and Gary Witherall

On 21 November 2002 Bonnie Witherall became a martyr for Christ when her life was suddenly taken by an unknown gunman who entered the prenatal clinic. Bonnie was preparing tea and cookies for the Palestinian refugee women that would be cared for that morning. She delighted in showing mercy and kindness to these Arab women and sharing the love of Jesus with them whenever she could.

Just a few months before her death, some friends visited Bonnie and her husband, Gary, where they lived and worked as missionaries in Sidon, Lebanon. They interviewed Bonnie on video, and she shared her struggle with fear and how the Lord and her husband helped her to overcome it. Here are Bonnie's own words:

On 11 September I came home from the clinic so
excited because that day I had had two or three
opportunities to tell people about Jesus. I was so
fired up. I felt as though I had a purpose here and
things were really great. Then I turned on the
news, and I saw it – I saw it live from here,
because it was four or five o'clock, which means it
was about nine in the morning there. I couldn't
believe it, and like all Americans I was in a state
of shock. But we had a little bit different perspective, because I had just spent the whole day
talking with and loving these Arab women,
showing them mercy and kindness; and that
night they were rejoicing in the Palestinian camp
that this had happened in America!

For us the real challenge was how to love these
people who you just really, honestly wanted to
hate! You can't fathom how much I just wanted to
turn my back on them and go back home. I
couldn't understand these people who would
rejoice so much over such loss and pain – especially people who had endured so much pain and
loss themselves. That was a real spiritual challenge for me, to get the resources from the Lord to
love these people who were so filled with joy over
the loss in the United States.

That first two weeks I didn't go out very much.
I didn't know if it was safe. I felt like everyone was
looking at me and knew I was an American. I felt
like I was a target for everybody. I was really fearful and really ready, not to go home, but definitely

ready to go to Beirut. Sidon is a lot more conserva-
tive and fundamental than Beirut.

I remember talking to my husband, Gary, one
night. I was in tears and trembling, and I said, 'I
can't handle it – I can't live like this.' Gary said to
me, 'Bonnie, there is nothing you can do to add a
day to your life, and there is nothing you can do
to take away one day.' He helped me to see that
every one of my days is written in God's plan,
and I can't do anything to change that. After he
said this I felt a release from this fear and a sense
of freedom to be able to walk down the streets of
Sidon, to be able to talk about Jesus, to be bolder
than I ever have been before, because I don't
know how long we will have here in Sidon. I
don't know how long we will be able to tell people about Jesus. I don't want something like 11
September to put so much fear in me that I am
disabled from doing what I've been called to do.
So I feel I've come a long way, and now I don't
have fear in that same way.

I still have fears about other things – obviously
I have a lot of issues in my life that God is still
working on – but as far as the terrorism/11
September issues, no, I'm not scared. I know that
God has my life in his hands and that I am where
he wants me to be right now. I'm confident of
that, and I'm happy to be here.

One more thing to remember is that every Arab
that I've met on the street has been very kind to
me. I just want to tell people to make friends with

Arabs. They are wonderful people. I feel so blessed and so honored to be in this part of the world – even after 11 September. I honestly wouldn't have wanted to be anywhere else, and I count it a privilege and a joy to be in the Middle East.

It's not always easy, and it's obviously hard to live in an uncertain place. You can't really put down roots, because you never know when you'll have to leave or be evacuated and things will spiral out of control. But I feel honored to know and to love Arabs, to eat and fellowship with them. I've really learned a lot, because I had no idea before I came! I had no Arab friends and no Muslim friends. I was scared as anything to go to the Muslim world. I had said to the Lord, 'I am never going to the Middle East. You can send me anywhere you want, but I'm not going to go there.' Until you expose yourself, it's very normal and natural for you to have those feelings, but I feel blessed that God called me here so that my views could change and I could experience what it is like to be friends with Arab people.

Bonnie is now in heaven, where she no longer has to deal with issues like fear. But what about her husband, Gary? How has all this affected his faith, his ministry and his life? I asked him those very things, and here is his response:

Bonnie was my best friend. We fell in love and enjoyed being with each other. We shared our joys, experiences and pain with each other. To know she is gone is devastation. My close friend is no longer there to share the road of life with me. I feel that everything is gone, and I have been thrown on to the Lord. The Lord has drawn close to me. I have fallen into his arms. He sustains me. He has comforted me, and I have survived in his presence. The pain of this tragedy is so enormous, yet the presence of God in my life has given peace.

It seems I am so alone, and yet the Lord's arms are around me, as I believe they are around Bonnie. I can do nothing other than trust with everything that is within me. Bonnie, my greatest treasure in life, is worthy of handing to Jesus, because what he has done for me is so great.

God prepared both of us for this tragedy. We both often talked about holding things and each other loosely. In doing this we were able to be living sacrifices. We were willing to even lay down our lives for the Kingdom. It is a life where Christ comes first. But this is a day-to-day thing. It is not a place you arrive. There is only today, and one cannot know what tomorrow will hold.

Fear and boldness are two words that are closely related. Fear is like oil that seeps into all the places of your life. It needs to be dealt with and renounced. Boldness comes to replace it. The question is, for what are you ready to lay down your precious life or the life of the one you love? These are questions that the American churches do not face. But in many places in the world, they are a daily reality that must be considered. I would rather burn brightly for Christ with risks than live a meaningless existence in a place regarded as safe. The safest place to be is where Jesus leads you, doing whatever he tells you to do – just ask Jonah.

The impact of Bonnie's death has been nothing short of stunning. As I share our story, I see how people are moved to deeper commitment and a willingness to serve. God's work through this situation silences me. I can do nothing except sit back and allow God to reign. I hope that thousands will respond to the life and death of Bonnie and go. Who will go to these lost fields where the costs can be so high? Lord, raise up men and women of faith!

Bonnie and Gary are wonderful examples of overcoming fear and being willing to do whatever God asks. Gary was able to encourage Bonnie past her fear after 11 September with the truth found in Psalm 139:16: 'You saw me before I was born. Every day of my life was recorded in your book. Every moment was laid out before a single day had passed' (NLT). Bonnie's death was not a tragic accident but part of God's plan for her and Gary's ministry. While this is not what Gary would have chosen, he has found the Lord sufficient to help him through this, and faithful to use it in meaningful and effective ways to further God's Kingdom – which is what Bonnie's life was and Gary's life is still all about.

* * *

The Testimonies of John and Jody

John and Jody are Americans who moved past their fears when they felt God calling them to serve in Afghanistan and, once there, found God to be very faithful in the midst of a very fearful situation.

We had good jobs but were restless in our hearts. We wondered if there might be a place somewhere where our skills could be used in missions. I [Jody] have been in clerical work most of my life, and John has been a design draftsman for farm machinery for over thirty years. As we looked into the possibilities, we were connected to a man who worked in South Asia for an agency that serves the people in Afghanistan in practical ways as a means of showing God's love.

We visited one country for two weeks and were very impressed with what different organisations were doing there. John was able to visit the work of this particular service agency in Afghanistan and was again impressed. We decided that if there were an opening for us we would like to serve there.

As we progressed through the application process, we were often asked questions like:

1) Why, at age sixty, would you want to go to a Third World country . . . and Afghanistan of all places? Aren't you afraid?
2) Why would you walk away from job security and the routine of work?
3) Why would you leave the security of home and family . . . at your age?

During this time of uncertainty, questioning and support raising a particular verse became very important to me:

Fear not; [there is nothing to fear] for I am with you; do not look around you in terror and be dismayed, for I am your God. I will strengthen and harden you to difficulties; yes, I will help you; yes, I will hold you up and retain you with My [victorious] right hand of righteousness and justice. (Isaiah 41:10, Amplified)

I posted this verse in my cubicle at work where I could see it every day. I posted it on the monitor of our computer at home where it could be seen often. This verse helped to answer those questions and calm my fears.

On 8 January 2001, we left to begin our work in Afghanistan. We had the privilege of trying to learn the language of Dari, establishing a new facility, and working as the personnel co-ordinator until 30 August.

At ten p.m., long after we had gone to bed on that very hot day, there was a persistent knock at the door. Our *chowkidar* (a watchman who protects the house and watches the gate) whispered to John that Taliban were at the gate. There were, in fact, three pickup truckloads of armed Taliban outside, with a group walking up the driveway, when John stepped outside to greet them. Seven of them entered our home and politely but firmly asked for all of our communication systems (a satellite phone and ham radio) and told us that we were under house arrest. Two armed Taliban would serve as guards at our gate, and we were not to leave the compound nor attempt to communicate with anyone. They left thirty minutes later, leaving the two guards with a couple of cots to sleep on.

John went down a few minutes later, taking the guards and the *chowkidar* each a bottle of ice-cold water for the night. We fed them the next day and a half and kept them refreshed with hot green tea and cold water. Two of our female team members were brought to our home on Friday with their luggage to stay the night. The following morning our director was brought with his luggage. We learned that all our offices and homes were sealed. We were put into our van, along with Taliban, and were escorted out of town to the

Afghan-Pakistan border where we had to walk across with only the possessions we could carry.

We were very surprised to be met at the border by journalists and photographers, and we learned from them that there had been an order from Khandahar that all the Christian NGOs (Non-Governmental Organisations, like ours) had to be out of the country that very day. We were the first out. We were very grateful that none of us were hurt or harassed.

We have since learned that most of our things were looted, stolen, gone. The offices, the guest-house and our personal homes are no longer available to us, and their furnishings and documents are gone. Following the 11 September attack on the United States, we were evacuated to Germany, where we all met together as a team to determine what our next steps should be. Everyone felt that we should regroup and continue the work of our Lord through this service organisation. Plans were established, and we all left for our home countries to explain to our supporters what had happened.

Does God keep his word? Previous to our expulsion, we had been in Kabul when Dayna Curry and Heather Mercer failed to show up at their homes at the end of the day. We learned that they, and then the rest of the Shelter Now International team, including their Afghan staff, were arrested. A Scripture became special to me that day in

August when we returned to the city, Psalm 94:20-23:

> Can a corrupt throne be allied with you – one that brings on misery by its decrees? They band together against the righteous and condemn the innocent to death. But the Lord has become my fortress, and my God the rock in whom I take refuge. He will repay them for their sins and destroy them for their wickedness; the Lord our God will destroy them.

All those who were arrested have since come out alive and well, and the Taliban government has been defeated.

The fears that we felt regarding our jobs, home, family, financial support, age, usefulness – and then when the Taliban came and took away our freedom and material possessions – these fears were all swallowed up in the words 'fear not.' God indeed strengthened us and helped us in our times of need.

Not only did God strengthen and help John and Jody with their fears during their ordeal but he also allowed them to overcome any fears about going back. Several months after they were forced to leave, John, Jody and the rest of their team were back in Afghanistan setting up their homes and restarting the projects they had been forced to abandon.

* * *

The Testimony of Hannah

Hannah, from the United States, had decided to give only one year to missions before she started college, but the Lord seemed to have other plans. He had some interesting ways of communicating his desires to her.

I am nineteen and came into missions immediately following high school. I served for one year in South Africa, and it was tremendous – life changing in so many ways. I could write pages and pages on that, but suffice it to say that my paradigm was certainly shifted! I had planned to start college after that first year of mission work and applied to four universities in the United States. Strangely enough, all four universities either turned me down or put me on their waiting list, and I was shocked! Coming from an advanced math and science high school, with a very good resumé, I should have been accepted easily.

I prayed about other possibilities, and the Lord definitely pointed out in some very interesting ways a ministry called Turning Point in London. As I began praying for some guidance, our team in South Africa was travelling to Cape Town for an outreach. There we visited some prisons, and as we were waiting to be released from one particular prison I glanced to my left and noticed a huge poster that read 'TURNING POINT'. This was referring to a prison programme, but what a shock!

Next, as I was reading a book, I stumbled across a line that just seemed to jump out at me: 'So Jesus had a *turning point* in his life.' I thought to myself, 'What is God trying to say here?'

One of the things that had been drawing me back home was a steady boyfriend, but a few weeks before all this confirmation stuff, he and I decided to just be friends, thus removing one obstacle.

I was praying one night, actually half-heartedly, when I decided to ask the Lord for one more bit of confirmation. After that time of prayer I was going to read a devotional book called *Experiencing God*, which our team was assigned to read as part of our training. I was a couple of months behind in my reading, but when I opened up to the proper page, the title of that day's devotion was 'A Turning Point!' On the page below, the phrase 'turning point' was mentioned about ten times. I thought to myself, 'This is it! God is really telling me something!'

So I called Turning Point and arranged to join them. Besides all the external signs the Lord gave me, the personal confirmation to me was the peace in my heart that this new decision brought.

Within two weeks of that phone call, all four universities wrote to say that they had made a mistake, and I was now accepted to attend. None the less, because the Lord had made it so clear, I went to Turning Point. Upon arriving in London, I heard that the Turning Point team had been praying for several months for people to help in the finance office, and I am a bookkeeper. Soon after my arrival a need arose for someone to work with kids and a musician, and that is exactly what I came there to do. God's timing is amazing when I look back at it.

So, if God wants you to go somewhere in missions for him, he will let you know in no uncertain terms. The catch? You have to be listening and available.

* * *

The Testimonies of David and Sandy

There are different methods and philosophies about raising support, from polished presentations to simply praying about needs, without talking about them, and trusting God to supply. David and Sandy, from the United States, were convinced that God had asked them to trust him to provide for their financial needs without making them known, but their faith was tested when they needed to raise a very large amount in a very short period of time.

The summer before we left for Central Asia was one of the most hectic we have ever experienced, for obvious reasons. But on top of getting ready to move, we were also working on adopting our second child from Mongolia, a land we had lived in for six years. Along with the money the mission leadership had suggested we raise (money for flying to Central Asia, setting up a home, and so on), we also needed funds to travel to Mongolia and pay all the fees necessary to adopt our daughter. My first estimates were that we needed around $12,000 to come in over the next two months, and as overwhelming as that figure was, it was what I had been praying for.

Things came to a head one day when my wife, Sandy, expressed some of her concerns regarding the financial picture. For years we had been following a principle we felt the Lord had given us – that we never solicit funds, only pray for them to come in. On this particular day Sandy wondered aloud if we should ask for help this one time, since we needed so much.

Her suggestion greatly disturbed me, and I went off to pray about it. I was walking down a road, opening up my heart, and said, 'Lord, I really need some encouragement regarding our finances today.' A split second after I prayed the word 'today', my eyes fell upon a bunch of pennies on the ground. Now, how many times in your life have you come across a bunch of change on the ground? And how many of those times were immediately after you had prayed about a financial need?

'Lord, I think we need a little bit more than a few pennies, but if this is how you want to start to provide, thank you.' I counted fifteen pennies. As I left that spot, the Lord's strategy came to me.

As soon as I got home, I gathered my wife and son together in the living room and told them what had happened and what I felt the Lord wanted us to do. Firstly, we were not to pray for $12,000 but for $15,000 to come in over the next two months – $1,000 for each penny I had found. Secondly, as the Lord answered the prayers, whenever $1,000 came in, we would transfer one of these pennies from one bowl to another bowl. And we would not tell anyone we were doing this. Each of us agreed and prayed together that the Lord would show us his power.

Over the next seven or eight weeks, as we prayed daily for this need, we transferred all fifteen of those pennies, each time making a ceremony of it. In fact, even more came in. The Lord is faithful!

From SCALING THE WALL
by KATHY HICKS
Copyright © 2003 Kathy Hicks, published by
Authentic Lifestyle
an imprint of Authentic Media
PO Box 300, Carlisle, Cumbria, CA3 0QS, UK
and PO Box 107, Waynesboro, GA30830, USA
www.paternoster-publishing.com

ISBN: 1-85078-538-4

J. JOHN

J. John is widely regarded as the most creative Christian speakers in the UK. His much-loved art of storytelling has helped thousands discover God and make more sense of everyday life.

He is author of a number of books including *The Life, Cool Christmas, Walking With God* and *Marriage Works*.

Epilogue – Social Concern

by J. John

Whose responsibility is it?

Seeking social justice would appear to be a fairly common concern. We sit on our sofas at home and are deeply moved by the sombre cries for help of charity appeals. Clips of small children hard at work in dangerous settings shock us; tales of trauma and life-long impoverishment stop us briefly in our tracks. We might even be spurred to donate some money occasionally when a particular cause grips our attention. But how shocked are we? How much does it filter through the immense cultural and social barriers that surround us, preventing us from completely relating and responding to the realities that face us?

Whatever our perception of the poverty crisis might be, the facts still remain clear:

❑ Almost every global environmental indicator has worsened over the last ten years and the gap between rich and poor is wider than ever. While over one billion people live on one dollar a day, people in developed countries are suffering from an epidemic of obesity.

❑ While 800 million are lacking the basic necessities for survival, we are spending money on weight-loss programs and cosmetic surgery.

❑ As our expectations of achievement levels, salary incomes and what we 'deserve' from life increase, so a fifth of the human race are condemned to make out a miserable existence without any possibility of self-improvement for themselves or their families.

We know the statistics . . . the facts remain clear.

We are also aware of the many public calls to counteract social inequalities; after World War II this was the driving cause and primary function of the new welfare state and continues to be the core basis for humanitarian charities all over the world, both Christian and secular. Theoretically, we have heard all of the problems and freely impart our full admiration to the aid and relief organisations that are at work. But how far do we see social concern as the work of these charities and to what extent is it my responsibility?

Just another human rights expression?

There is a problem with looking at social concern in isolation. That is, that in our minds it can so easily become just another promotion of rights, sitting alongside protests for gay marriages in churches, bitter demands of the unemployed or a march for the fox hunting ban to be lifted. For us individually, social concern takes on a new level of importance when viewed in the context of Christianity. Without the motivation and model of Christ's compassion and love for the poor, 'social justice' can become the arid call of just another group of dissidents: forlorn of hope and full of pessimistic resentments.

On the other side of the coin, social justice is a necessary part of the outworking of our Christian faith. They are integral parts of one another and together they combine the 'works' and the 'faith' without which neither means very much. Jesus taught that both the vertical and horizontal relationships are of equal importance; our response to God and each other.

Why should it be such a priority for us?

There are several reasons practically why social concern is so important.

1. It is a channel for evangelism. Before the gospel-telling part of evangelism, it can be a link; building bridges, breaking down prejudices and opening doors. Once people's 'felt needs' are clearly the area of your concern, their 'spiritual needs' may reveal themselves and the Holy Spirit may be allowed to work.

2. It is a way of showing God's love to a desperate world. Even if no bridges were built by social actions, there would still be reasons to be concerned with social justice. Revealing the love of God was Jesus' main priority and conversions were of secondary importance.

   Jesus Christ . . . gave himself for us to redeem us from all wickedness and to purify for himself a people that are his very own, eager to do what is good. (Tit. 2:14)

3. It is a way for us to learn to love. Social concern is so important as it is an opportunity for us to show the love that God commands us to have. This 'love' should not express itself in a distant sigh of sympathy or in an uncomfortable pang of guilt as we read about circumstances so far from our own. When we have faith, we are called on to 'do,' not merely to feel or even to empathise with, but to act.

'Loving' one another calls us to struggle against everything that condemns people to a sub-human existence – hunger, disease, poverty, inequality and injustice. The church must exhibit an obvious concern for all segments of society, for all are to share in the Kingdom of God.

Speaking in common terms

To the world, Christians may be a strange bunch! We might not always enjoy the same kind of fun or conversation as other people. We may seem to enjoy church services and tend to meet on a Wednesday night to discuss the Bible instead of going to the pub. Our theology to them may appear incomprehensible and our ideas perplexing. Some may warm to us and some may not. Whatever their views, we have the ability to speak in a language that is universally understood: that of compassion and justice. We know that unbelievers are not convinced about God's goodness by church-going or even meaningful words outside of church. A positive impact is made by programmes attempting to better the condition of the disadvantaged and neglected – showing a practical love.

An international research organisation conducted a world-wide survey on the leaders in the past that had made a difference and who could not be ignored. Two names came at the top of the list: Mother Teresa and Desmond Tutu. Compassion and justice are the real language understood by the world.

Why does poverty exist?

Even when we have all sorts of theories clearly set out in our minds, this question still plagues us. Some people see poverty as a self-inflicted wound caused by a mixture of lack of effort, mismanagement and bad luck. Others see poverty as linked to deficiencies, weaknesses and maladjustments of families, and suggest that children are trained to repeat the failure, delinquency, crime and immorality of those nearest to them – 'the sins of the fathers are visited upon the next generation'. A third view is that poverty is enforced by the rich and powerful in order to maintain the status quo.

Whichever you may deem to be true, individual examples soon multiply. A group of individuals soon form a ghetto, a ghetto soon become a region, and a region can soon become a whole country or even a group of countries.

In classic economic terms, a person's income reflects his or her competitive worth. People are responsible individually for their actions and conditions, and therefore monetary rewards go to those with talent and effort.

However, individuals are only part of a wider economic picture; if a community's resources are run down, even those with talent and effort may be forced to go down with it. The whole group can become one, almost doomed to material failure.

A biblical perspective of the poor

However many geographical reports, scientific conclusions or government assessments we absorb, we will find that the biblical perspective of the poor is very different.

The Old Testament uses several different Hebrew words when referring to the poor: *ani* is the most common word, used seventy-seven times. *ani* literally means 'a person bowed down', someone who has to look up to others on whom he or she is dependent. It is interesting that the ani are not contrasted with the rich, but with the oppressor who tends to keep the ani in the position that they are in.

A second word to describe the poor in the Bible is *anaw*, which is used eighteen times and refers to people who feel they have little value or worth before God. A third term, *ebyon*, is used sixty times and refers to the situation of 'beggars.'

These words – *ani, anaw* and *ebyon* – are full of emotion. They are not neutral words, but words that call for urgent change. In the beginning, as God created the world, there was no distinction between the rich and the poor; the word 'poor' does not emerge in the book of Genesis. Abraham exemplifies this unproblematic view of riches. In this period, riches were those of the whole 'tribe' – if one was rich, then the whole tribe was rich.

Lowly, needy, simple-minded, insignificant, weak and oppressed – these are some of the meanings of the most frequently used New Testament terms. There are references to the social conditions of the time and much talk of landowners, slaves, and honest and dishonest stewards. The tensions and problems of extremes between the rich and the poor are clearly identified with.

In its variety of terms and expressions, the Bible encapsulates a much wider circumference of those who require our attention – not just the 'materially' poor included by the lists of government statistics.

We have drugs for people with diseases like leprosy. But these drugs do not treat the main problem, the disease of being unwanted. That's what my sisters hope to provide. The sick and poor suffer even more from rejection than material want. Loneliness and the feeling of being unwanted is the most terrible poverty.

Mother Teresa

We need never consider ourselves in the wrong position to be able to make a difference. Overseas missionary work may seem too daunting, but is just one of countless opportunities to act on social concern. The openings are so clear in under-developed countries, but also apparent sometimes right in front of us.

The Reverend Marie Elizabeth Dyer, a hospital chaplain, writes of her experience:

> I already knew I was not an evangelist. I did not feel called upon to baptise all nations, nor all peoples. I learned to love more deeply and to hold this commandment primary in my life. One day I was reading Matthew 25:35-36, 'for I was hungry and you gave me something to eat, I was thirsty and you gave me something to drink, I was a stranger and you invited me in. I needed your clothes and you clothed me, I was sick and you looked after me. I was in prison and you came to visit me.'

Marie began to interpret these verses in a new way because she knew the hunger, thirst, nakedness and imprisonment of her patients. So she wrote:

> I was hungry ...
> . . . for a new life away from the pressures of an alcoholic husband – you did not give me a life away, but new ways to live with my man;

. . . for breath that would not make me gasp – I continued to gasp but you stayed, I knew that you cared;

. . . for company, for I am the only one in this room without visitors – you brought me a flower, laughed at my jokes and read scripture to me.

I was thirsty . . .
. . . for the knowledge of a diagnosis – you helped me to face whatever I heard;
. . . for righteousness, a sense of forgiveness in life – I knew that you believed and I began to believe too;
. . . for hope that a loved one would indeed not die – you left me with hope and promised to stay by my side.

I was a stranger . . .
. . . for I did not speak English – Thank you, you tried to communicate and did not just smile and then walk away.
. . . I had never been in a hospital before, I felt not only strange, but terrified – you believed my fear, you prayed with me too.

I was naked . . .
. . . for I was a doctor, my inability to express feelings was exposed by your words – and you put a hand on my shoulder to tell me you knew that I cared;

. . . for I was old, my veins and even my bones stick out – you clothed my skin with loving caresses;

. . . for my grief showed all over my face – you did not avoid me, but sat down to talk.

I was sick . . .
. . . and you visited me.

I was in prison in the loneliness of being unmarried – you told me you remembered the hardness of such days; in a room with no windows – together we shared . . .

Working for justice and Jesus

He has taken upon himself the form of a servant.
(Phil. 2:7)

To be a Christian is to be open to the rest of the world, not as a master, but as a servant. Working for God is to be working for justice. God has called us all individually to take responsibility and to work for social justice in his world. The blessings and gifts that we enjoy in our lives are not ours to keep to ourselves, but to share and to give them away – in whatever form that might take.

Martin of Tours was a Roman soldier and a Christian. One cold winter day, as he was entering a city, a beggar stopped him and asked for alms. Martin had no money, but the beggar was blue and shivering with cold, and Martin gave what he had. He took off his soldier's coat, worn and frayed as it was; he cut it in two and gave half to the beggar man. That night he had a dream. In it he saw the heavenly places and all the angels and Jesus in the midst of them. Jesus was wearing half of a Roman soldier's coat. One of the angels said to him, 'Master, why are you wearing that battered old coat? Who gave it to you?' And Jesus answered softly, 'My servant Martin gave it to me.'

The way forward

Be inspired by this book and the tales of courageous people working for Jesus. Whatever our circumstances, we can always go somewhere, even if it seems only one small step of the way. Moreover, we have God to help us do that. To quote Mother Teresa when she worked in Calcutta:

We try to pray through our work by doing it with Jesus, for Jesus, to Jesus. That helps us put our whole heart and soul into doing it. The dying, the crippled, the mentally ill, the unwanted, the unloved – they are Jesus in disguise.

There is so much that we can do and, while no person can change the world, we can still change the world for one person! We can be encouraged because however little we consider our gifts to be, everything we have can be used for the Kingdom. Just consider the words of the eighteenth-century philosopher Edmund Burke:

> Nobody made a greater mistake than he who did nothing because he could only do a little.